Table of Contents

Note to Parents and Teachers 4
Introduction to Presidential Elections 5-8
Who Is Eligible to President 10-12
The Oath of Office and the Responsibilities of the President. 13-15
Term Limits 16-17
Voting Laws—then and now 18-21
Political Parties 22-27
    Federalist
    Democratic-Republicans
    Democrats
    Whigs
    Republicans
On the Campaign Trail 28-34
First in the Nation: The Iowa Caucus and
the New Hampshire Primary 34-37
The Conventions 38-44
The Vice Presidential Pick 45-48
Historic Campaigns 49-52
Campaigning in the Television Age 53-55
Public Opinion Polls 56-59
The Electoral College 60-63
Election Day 64-67
Notable Elections 68-71
Inauguration Day 72-74

Appendix:
The Elections 75-85
The Presidents 86-94

Projects:
Building a Platform with Planks 95-105
The Campaign Game 104-107

Glossary 108-110
Answer Key 110-112

WITHDRAWN

Dear Parents and Teachers,

This book includes text and activities to help students understand the election cycle that takes place every four years for the Presidency of the United States. It all begins with the announcement by each candidate and the beginning of each campaign to raise money, awareness, and votes. This quadrennial event is the biggest prize for elected office and usually lasts up to two years before the actual November balloting.

This book is written to help explain the winner-take-all electoral system laid out in the United States Constitution. The process of electing our president every four years in the United States is a rough and tumble political blood sport—the candidates play to win.

From the very beginning of each and every campaign, the candidates know that to win, they have to craft the message that will resonate with the most people. They have to study the issues relevant to the times— the economy, external security threats, taxes, and social issues. Each candidate then has to identify backers who will donate money to their campaigns and help them raise the millions of dollars it takes to mount a credible race first for the nomination of their party. After that race is won, it is a hard fought race for the highest elected office in the United States in November.

This book is made up of 17 small chapters. Each chapter is broken into two parts—the text, which will explain a concept or event in the race to the White House, and then the second part which consists of an activity or project, to deepen the understanding or a review that will test comprehension. Some of these reviews are fill in the blank, some are brief essay, and some are matching. The book starts with the basics—the constitutional qualifications. Race to the White House lays out the entire process starting with the announcement, through the primary and caucus voting system to the nominating convention. It also highlights some of our notable elections and how some presidents were elected without winning the popular vote—in 1876, 1888, and in 2000. In addition there is a section about how our voting laws and who is eligible to vote has changed since our first election of George Washington. Then ends with the November balloting and the Electoral College process.

This book takes the student from the nomination process and follows the candidate all the way through to Inauguration Day. Let the race begin!

Introduction to Presidential Elections

Words to look for

Candidates   Caucus   Election Day   Political party

Slogan   Primary   United States Constitution

Every four years there is a race to the White House—that is candidates vying to see who will win the presidency. But not everyone is qualified to be President of the United States. The qualifications, however, are simple and laid out in the United States Constitution in Article II, Section 1; it says:

> *No person except a natural born citizen, or a citizen of the United States, at the time of the adoption of this Constitution, shall be eligible to the office of President; neither shall any person be eligible to that office who shall not have attained to the age of thirty-five years, and been fourteen years a resident within the United States.*

Every four years in the BIG race candidates from both of the major political parties and smaller and lesser known political parties run to hold the highest elected position in our government. Political parties are groups of people who are bound together because they have the same beliefs and have the same goal in mind—to elect a person from their political party to the presidency.

Election Day takes place on the first Tuesday after the first Monday in November every four years. But, the running starts well before the general election.

Candidates from many political parties announce their candidacies for office. Then they go about trying to win the nomination of their political party so they can run in the general election.

The youngest person to take the office of president was Theodore Roosevelt, who was the sitting Vice President of the United States when President William McKinley was assassinated. According to the succession laws, the Vice President then became president. Teddy Roosevelt was 42 years and 322 days old. The youngest person to be elected president was John Fitzgerald Kennedy at age 43 years and 236 days old.

The first campaigns did not resemble what we have now. In the first place it was considered to be beneath the candidates to go out and campaign for oneself. So, rival newspapers and advocates or surrogates did the campaigning on behalf of the candidates. That began to change in the mid-1800s when political parties became more aggressive about trying to get their candidates elected.

In a time when there was no radio or television, mass communication boiled down to the newspaper. Campaigns would organize torch-light parades and campaign sloganeering. One of the first campaign slogans extolled Andrew Jackson's military career, "The Hero of New Orleans". One of the most famous campaign slogans was rolled out in 1840 on behalf of William Henry Harrison, "Tippecanoe and Tyler Too" which originated from a song called Tipp and Ty. Tippecanoe was a famous battle led by William Henry Harrison against the Shawnee Chief Tecumseh and a band of his warriors in 1811; Tyler was John Tyler, the vice-presidential candidate running with Harrison.

In 1844 James Knox Polk ran on expanding the U.S. territory further North with a slogan of "54-40 or Fight". In 1856, the Republican Party, in their first presidential contest, chose John Fremont as their candidate. The political fight at the time was the decision whether Kansas would be a free state or a slave state; John Fremont campaigned on "Free Soil, Free Labor, and Fremont".

Following are some of the slogans from the past 120 years of presidential elections:

1896
"Prosperity at Homes, Prestige Abroad" and "Patriotism, Protection, and Prosperity"-William McKinley
"No Crown of Thorns, No Cross of Gold" William Jennings Bryan

1900
"Four more years of the full dinner pail" William McKinley

1904
"Square Deal" Theodore Roosevlet

1916
"He kept us out of war" Woodrow Wilson

1920
Return to Normalcy" Warren Harding

1924
"Keep Cool and Keep Coolidge" Calvin Coolidge

1928
"Who but Hoover?" and "A chicken in every pot and a car in every garage" Herbert Hoover

1932
"Happy Days Are Here Again" and "A New Deal for the American people" Franklin Roosevelt
"We are turning the corner" Herbert Hoover.

1936
"Let's Get Another Deck" Alfred M. Landon

1940
"Win with Willkie" Wendell L. Willkie
"Better A Third Term" Franklin Roosevelt

1944
"Don't swap horses in midstream" Franklin Roosevelt.

1948
"I'm just wild about Harry" and "Fair Deal" Harry Truman

1952
"I Like Ike" Eisenhower
"The Experienced Candidate" Adlai Stevenson

1956
"I still like Ike" Dwight D. Eisenhower

1960

"A time for greatness" and We Can Do Better" John Fitzgerald Kennedy
"Experience Counts" Richard Nixon

1964

"All the way with LBJ" and "The stakes are too high for you to stay at home." Lyndon Johnson
"In Your Heart, You Know He's Right" Barry Goldwater

1968

"Some talk change. Others cause it." Hubert Humphrey
"Nixon's the One Nixon" and "This time, vote like your whole world depended on it" Richard Nixon.

1972

"Nixon Now More Than Ever" Richard Nixon

1976

"He's making us proud again" Gerald Ford
"A Leader, For a Change" Jimmy Carter

1980

"Are You Better Off Than You Were Four Years Ago?" Ronald Reagan
"It's a Matter of Values." Jimmy Carter

1984

It's Morning Again in America — Ronald Reagan Slogan for 1984 Presidential Election
"Where the Beef?" Walter Mondale

1988

"Kinder, Gentler Nation" George H. W. Bush

1992

"It's the economy, stupid" and "Don't Stop Thinking about Tomorrow" Bill Clinton
"Ross for Boss" H. Ross Perot
"The Better Man for a Better America" Bob Dole

1996

"Building a bridge to the twenty-first century" Bill Clinton

2000

"Prosperity and Progress" Al Gore

Kinder, Gentler Nation" and "Reformer with Results" George W. Bush

2004

"A Safer World and a More Hopeful America" George W. Bush
"A Stronger America" John Kerry

2008

"Change we can believe in" and "Yes We Can" Barrack Obama
"Country First" John McCain

2012

"Forward" Barack Obama.
"Believe in America" Mitt Romney

The candidates campaign full throttle trying to pick up votes during the caucuses and primaries. To win the party's nomination, each candidate has to amass a certain number of delegates to the national convention. Once the candidate wins the nomination at the national convention, they move to the general election. On the first Tuesday in November every four years, the national election for the presidency is held.

Name _____

Review 1:

Read each question below and answer the question:

1. What three qualifications are necessary to become president?

_____

_____

_____

2. How did candidates campaign before electronic media?

_____

_____

_____

3. Who was the youngest person to become president?   _____

4. Who was the youngest person elected president?   _____

5. Explain why the answers to questions 3 and 4 are not the same.

_____

_____

_____

_____

Name _____

Identify that Slogan!

Look at the drawings below and identify which campaign slogan these cartoons illustrate.

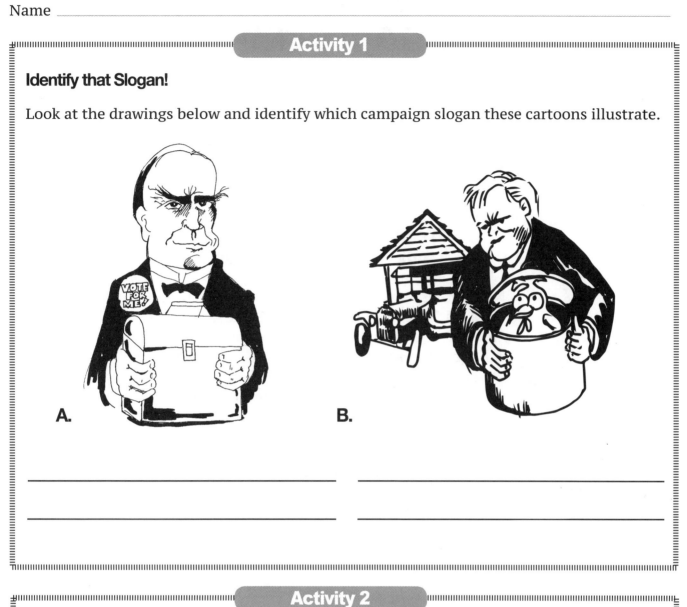

A. _____

_____

B. _____

_____

Match that Slogan

Read each slogan below and match it to the president who used it in his campaign.

1. _____ Fair Deal   a. Franklin Roosevelt

2. _____ Square Deal   b. Alfred Landon

3. _____ New Deal   c. Harry Truman

4. _____ Change the Deck   d. Theodore Roosevelt

Who is eligible to be President?

To run for president each candidate has to meet certain requirements laid out by the United States Constitution.

The United States Constitution, Article II, Section 1. It states

No person except a natural born citizen, or a citizen of the United States, at the time of the adoption of this Constitution, shall be eligible to the office of President; neither shall any person be eligible to that office who shall not have attained to the age of thirty-five years, and been fourteen years a resident within the United States.

Two of the qualifications for the presidency are easy enough to check—age, and length that a person has resided in the country. The first qualification listed in the constitution, however, is much more difficult to define—natural born citizen.

Natural-born citizen

Who is a natural-born citizen? The 14th Amendment defines citizenship this way:

"All persons born or naturalized in the United States, and subject to the jurisdiction thereof, are citizens of the United States and of the State wherein they reside."

U.S. Code, Chapter 12, Subchapter III, Part 1, Section 1401 describes Nationals and Citizens of the United States at birth in the following way:

The following shall be nationals and citizens of the United States at birth:

(a) a person born in the United States, and subject to the jurisdiction thereof;

(b) a person born in the United States to a member of an Indian, Eskimo, Aleutian, or other aboriginal tribe: Provided, That the granting of citizenship under this subsection shall not in any manner impair or otherwise affect the right of such person to tribal or other property;

(c) a person born outside of the United States and its outlying possessions of parents both of whom are citizens of the United States and one of whom has had a residence in the United States or one of its outlying possessions, prior to the birth of such person;

(d) a person born outside of the United States and its outlying possessions of parents one of whom is a citizen of the United States who has been physically present in the United States or one of its outlying possessions for a continuous period of one year prior to the birth of such person, and the other of whom is a national, but not a citizen of the United States;

(e) a person born in an outlying possession of the United States of parents one of whom is a citizen of the United States who has been physically present in the United States or one of its outlying possessions for a continuous period of one year at any time prior to the birth of such person;

(f) a person of unknown parentage found in the United States while under the age of five years, until shown, prior to his attaining the age of twenty-one years, not to have been born in the United States;

(g) a person born outside the geographical limits of the United States and its outlying possessions of parents one of whom is an alien, and the other a citizen of the United States who, prior to the birth of such person, was physically present in the United States or its outlying possessions for a period or periods totaling not less than five years, at least two of which were after attaining the age of fourteen years: Provided, That any periods of honorable service in the Armed Forces of the United States, or periods of employment with the United States Government or with an international organization as that term is defined in section 288 of title 22 by such citizen parent, or any periods during which such citizen parent is physically present abroad as the dependent unmarried son or daughter and a member of the household of a person

    (A) honorably serving with the Armed Forces of the United States, or
    (B) employed by the United States Government or an international organization as defined in section 288 of title 22, may be included in order to satisfy the physical-presence requirement of this paragraph. This proviso shall be applicable to persons born on or after December 24, 1952, to the same extent as if it had become effective in its present form on that date; and

(h) a person born before noon (Eastern Standard Time) May 24, 1934, outside the limits and jurisdiction of the United States of an alien father and a mother who is a citizen of the United States who, prior to the birth of such person, had resided in the United States.

Who is Qualified? Review

In the 2008 election there were two questions about whether or not the candidates were qualified under the United States code to be president. Read each scenario and answer the question.

1. In 2008, Arizona Senator John McCain ran for president on the Republican ticket. At the time of his birth, August 29, 1936, his father, John S. McCain was stationed in the Panama Canal Zone. John McCain was born at the Coco Solo Naval Air Station in the Panama Canal Zone, which was under the control of the United States. According to what you have read in the code about being a natural-born citizen, was Senator John McCain qualified to be president? Explain your answer.

_____

_____

_____

_____

_____

2. Illinois Senator Barrack Obama ran for president on the Democratic ticket. At the time of the election, some did not believe that he was qualified to be president. Some believed that Obama was not actually born in the United States; others believed he was not qualified to be president because his father was a native-born Kenyan and not a naturalized citizen. However, at the time of his birth, his mother Stanley Ann Dunham Obama gave birth to Barack on August 4, 1961, at the Kapi'olan Maternity and Gynecological Hospital at Honolulu, Hawaii. According to what you have read in the code about being a natural-born citizen, was Senator Barack Obama qualified to be president? Explain your answer.

_____

_____

_____

_____

_____

The Oath of Office and the responsibilities of the President

Words to look for

Oath   Affirm

The United States Constitution Article Two, Section One, Clause Eight:

Before he enter on the Execution of his Office, he shall take the following Oath or Affirmation:— *"I do solemnly swear (or affirm) that I will faithfully execute the Office of President of the United States, and will to the best of my Ability, preserve, protect and defend the Constitution of the United States."*

Since George Washington first took the oath on the balcony of Federal Hall at New York City on April 30, 1789, every president has taken this oath because it is mandated by the United States Constitution--Article Two, Section One, Clause Eight. George Washington was sworn into office by Robert Livingston, the Chancellor of New York. At the time, the Chancellor was the highest judicial office in the state. As has become the custom most presidents have been sworn in by the Chief Justice of the United States even though the Constitution does not designate who should administer the oath of office. Only one president was not sworn in by a judge of one kind or another and that was President Calvin Coolidge. Upon learning about the death of Warren Harding, then Vice President Coolidge was sworn in by his father, John Calvin Coolidge, Sr. who was a notary public.

Lyndon Baines Johnson was the only president who was sworn in by a woman. President John F. Kennedy and Vice President Lyndon Johnson were in Dallas, Texas, on a campaign swing through the state when an assassin shot President Kennedy. Upon the death of President Kennedy, Johnson assumed the office--Sarah T. Hughes, a U.S. District Court Judge, swore Johnson into office on Air Force One, the President's official plane.

With the exception of President Franklin Pierce each president has used the word "swear" instead "affirm".

The president, once elected is the head of the executive branch of government—the United States Government is divided into three branches—the legislative, the judicial, and the executive branch. The legislative branch is divided into two houses—the House of Representatives and the Senate, these two houses have the power to write laws. The judicial branch makes up the court system which interprets the law. The executive branch carries out the laws that Congress (the House and the Senate) passes.

The President has five Responsibilities:

Military

The President of United States is also the commander in chief of our armed forces. He leads our forces and determines if troops should be sent into battle. In our form of government a civilian heads the military.

Legislative

The President takes an oath to faithfully execute the office of the presidency. In real terms that means that he or she will enforce the laws passed by Congress.

The President also has a role in laws that get passed and laws that don't get passed. For example, the President can recommend laws and can veto laws that are passed by both houses. If a President vetoes a law both houses of have to override the veto with a vote of ¾ of its members.

Diplomatic

The chief diplomatic officer of the United States is the President. The President has meetings with other heads of state and negotiates treaties, or agreements with other countries. The President also appoints ambassadors who serve in the U.S. embassies around the world. The Senate has to confirm (or approve) the nominees for those positions and the Senate has to approve the treaties negotiated by the President.

Judicial

While the President does not adjudicate court cases, he does appoint judges to the bench. All Federal judges are appointed by the President. Once a President nominates a person to a judgeship, the Senate must approve the person before they take the appointment to serve.

Chief Executive

The President is the head of the Executive Branch of the government. As such, he appoints people to head the various executive functions such as: The Department of Education, Agriculture, Commerce, etc.

Name _____

The Oath of Office and the responsibilities of the President Review

1. What person swears in the President?

   _____

2. Define oath.

   _____

   _____

   _____

3. List the three branches of government:

   _____

   _____

   _____

4. Name five of the President's responsibilities:

   _____

   _____

   _____

   _____

   _____

Term Limits

US Constitution, Amendment XXII, Section 1
(ratified February 27, 1951)

Section 1. No person shall be elected to the office of the President more than twice, and no person who has held the office of President, or acted as President, for more than two years of a term to which some other person was elected President shall be elected to the office of the President more than once. But this article shall not apply to any person holding the office of President when this article was proposed by the Congress, and shall not prevent any person who may be holding the office of President, or acting as President, during the term within which this article becomes operative from holding the office of President or acting as President during the remainder of such term.

Section 2. This article shall be inoperative unless it shall have been ratified as an amendment to the Constitution by the legislatures of three-fourths of the several states within seven years from the date of its submission to the states by the Congress.

George Washington was our first president and as such set a precedent of only serving two terms. Though it was not codified into law, this precedent was followed for a century and a half. Not until Franklin Delano Roosevelt ran for a successful third term in 1940 was Washington's precedent broken. In 1944, Roosevelt ran again and was elected to a 4th term.

Thomas Jefferson, James Madison, James Monroe, Andrew Jackson, and Ulysses Grant all followed the precedent that George Washington set. However, two presidents, Grover Cleveland and Woodrow Wilson did seek a third term but neither were successful.

In 1947, the 80th Congress proposed and approved the 22nd Amendment. After it was approved by Congress it went to the states for ratification. Three-fourths of the states' legislatures approved the amendment in early 1951, which meant it had been adopted as an amendment to the Constitution restricting presidents to two terms.

Term Limits

1. How many terms can a president serve?

_____

2. What amendment to the Constitution limits the term of a president?

_____

3. Which president set the precedent of serving only two terms?

_____

4. Which president broke the precedent of serving two terms?

_____

5. Under the amendment to the Constitution, can a person be elected president to terms if tthey became president upon the death of a president one year into that president's term? Explain your answer.

_____

_____

_____

_____

Introduction to Presidential Elections

Words to look for

Ratify   Mandate   Emancipated

Reconstruction   Jim Crow Laws

It took the United States government over 200 years to develop equitable laws for all its citizens. This is because the voting laws had not been fully addressed in the Constitution and the specifics of who was allowed to vote fell upon each state to govern and control.

As late as the twentieth century, the largest groups barred from voting were women, African Americans, Native Americans, and the poor! It took several amendments to ratify the Constitution to insure the rights of every eligible citizen who was 18 years old, or above, regardless of race, religion, gender, economic status, or age. But, to understand how voting rights evolved one must look at the history of the United States.

In the early colonial days between 1600 and 1776, Christian groups influenced the laws and mandated that voting requirements be given to only Anglo men who owned 50 acres or more of land or property. These lucky few paid substantial taxes to their community, church and the British crown. Anyone else, including Catholics and Jewish people, regardless if they owned property, were barred from voting in several of the colonies.

Once the Constitution was written in 1787, some of the newly formed states allowed men who served in the army or militias, their right to vote. Vermont was the most progressive of all the states because it was the first to eliminate the taxpaying and property tax requirements. When all states finally eliminated the religious requirements, 60 to 70 percent of adult Anglo men were able to vote.

African Americans and Minorities

Prior to the Civil War, African Americans living in the southern slave owning states were considered property. In 1863, President Abraham Lincoln emancipated the Southern slaves with the 13th Amendment to the Constitution. While these slaves were freed most were illiterate and did not own property. By 1868, the Constitution was again changed with the 14th Amendment that allowed 21-year old males the right to vote- even if they did not own property. This amendment did not guarantee the rights of African Americans because it did not address "color" and race issues. But a few years later this issue was somewhat resolved with the 15th Amendment as it extended the right for men of all races the right to vote.

After the Civil War, the Reconstruction of the South began and with it came Jim Crow laws that segregated African Americans from the white population. The Southern States: Alabama, Georgia, Louisiana, Mississippi, North Carolina, South Carolina, Texas, and Virginia had enacted poll taxes and literacy laws that restricted African American, Native Americans, and all poor citizens, including white people, their rights to vote. Almost 100 years went by when a huge effort to bring these illegal practices and obvious discrimination to light. In 1965, Dr. Martin Luther King launched a voter registration drive in Selma, Alabama. For seven weeks King led hundreds of Selma's African American residents to register to vote. Nearly 2,000 black demonstrators, including Dr. King, were jailed for their efforts. Then, a young African American man was murdered and Dr. King called for a march from Selma to the state capital of Montgomery, Alabama. The massive group of demonstrators crossed a bridge and 200 state police attacked them with tear gas, nightsticks, and whips. With undaunted courage the march resumed but this time the marchers had federal protection. On March 25, an astounding crowd of 25,000 gathered at the state capitol and Dr. Martin Luther King Jr., gave a speech to the crowd in which he demanded an end to poverty, segregated schools, and voter discrimination.

As a result of Dr. King's efforts and others, two measures were adopted to safeguard the voting rights of African Americans. The first was the 24th Amendment that barred all states from controlling the votes with poll taxes. But after a century of deliberate and violent denial of African Americans rights, President Johnson signed the Voting Rights Act. This law is often held up as the most effective civil rights law ever enacted.

The 24th Amendment and the Voting Rights Act also helped other minorities who had been shut out of the voting process because they were poor and oftentimes, illiterate. It is important to note that while American Indians were the indigenous people of this country, they were never considered citizens of the United States. In the late 1880's many Native Americans were told that they could be citizens if they gave up their tribal affiliations, but this still did not guarantee their right to vote. American Indian's civil rights had to be fought for by luminaries of the day such as Dr. Carlos Montezuma. His words brilliant words, pleas and demands for American Indians citizenship and their right to vote, came one year after his death in 1924. The Indian Citizenship Act grants all Native Americans the rights of citizenship, including the right to vote in federal elections.

Women's Suffrage

As early as 1848, women began rallying for their Constitutional rights in Seneca Falls, New York. For decades they continued to fight for their voting rights by coordinating parades and demonstrations that often came with physical attacks, mistreatment and even jail. Eventually, fifteen states had granted full voting rights to women but most women across the nation had a longer wait. After a sometimes violent struggle, the Constitution was ratified with the 19th Amendment and in 1920 women finally won their right to vote.

Change Continues

Voting rights for United States citizens continues to be in flux. Additional amendments and laws have been changed to meet the needs of all citizens. The 23rd Amendment was ratified in 1961. Until that time, those living in the District of Columbia (which is not a state) were not allowed to vote. Furthermore, in 1971, the 26th Amendment was ratified to change the voting age from 21 to 18. The idea was that if one could be drafted at 18 to fight in a war for the country and it's citizens, then they were old enough to vote.

Voting Laws-Then and Now

The Constitution never determined who was allowed to vote so it was originally decided by the individual states. Because of state and local discriminatory practices the federal government eventually stepped in and instituted several amendments to the Constitution and legislation.

*14th Amendment was ratified in 1868.

Affirms: That any eligible 21 year old male has the right to vote even if they did not own property.

*15th Amendment was ratified in 1870.

Affirms: That a man cannot be denied their right to vote on "account of race, color, or previous condition of servitude."

* 17th Amendment was ratified in 1913.

Affirms: that members of the U.S. Senate would be directly elected by the people instead of the State Legislatures, as had been done in the past.

* The 19th Amendment was ratified in 1920.

Affirms: The right to vote could not be denied on "account of sex." Until this time, few states allowed women their rights. The State of Wyoming was one of the more progressive states that allowed women their rights long before the rest of the nation.

*23rd Amendment was ratified in 1961.

Affirms: That the citizens from the District of Columbia had the right to vote in the Presidential and vice-presidential elections.

*24th Amendment ratified in 1964.

Affirms: That states could not require their citizens to pay a poll tax in federal elections. Most people had believed that the tax was meant to discourage the poor, and particularly poor African Americans and American Indians, from voting.

*26th Amendment was ratified in 1971.

Affirms: That the voting age is lowered from 21 yeas of age to 18 years age for national, state and local elections.

Voting Laws-Then and Now

1. Review the sequence of time and the amendments that were ratified to the Constitution regarding voting rights. Consider who has been left behind in the voting rights debate. Are there segments of the population that have been left out today? For example, there are the homeless or disenfranchised citizens who may want to vote even though they have no permanent addresses. Recent debates also include whether or not felons, who have served their time, be allowed to vote. Some states allow felons to petition to have their rights restored after they have served their time.

_____

_____

2. Make an argument "for" or "against" voting rights for other segments of the population. Ask your parents for their points of views. Or, contact your state representative and ask for their ideas on the subject.

_____

_____

_____

3. Look at other countries and their voting rights laws. Ask yourself if they are the same or different and why. Is everyone allowed to vote? If not, who is left out?

_____

_____

_____

4. Finally, and most important, what are your thoughts on voting rights for you? Some believe that voting not only a right but also a privilege. Explain why you agree or disagree?

_____

_____

_____

_____

Political Parties

In spite of Washington's warning against political parties the factions in the early history of America grew into political parties.

The first two political parties were the Though, Washington is often considered and had no political party affiliation. Hamilton led the nascent Federalist central government. They were American Revolution, each colony, of the United up war costs. The policies included the bank and paying off the from the Revolutionary elected was John Adams,

Federalists and the Democratic-Republicans. a Federalist, he eschewed political parties However, his Treasury Secretary Alexander Party. The Federalist favored a strong pro-British in foreign policy. During the which became states after the ratification Constitution, had racked Federalists' financial formation of a national debts that the states owed War. The only Federalist who was a one-termed president.

The third president, Thomas Republican. That party through most of the 1820s James Monroe, and John Quincy president. However, the coalition fell apart the National Republicans and the Democrats.

Jefferson, was a Democratic- held the presidency from 1800 with Jefferson, James Madison, Adams all being elected breaking into two parties—

Andrew Jackson won in 1832, securing the Democratic Party a place in American history. Out of the ashes of the Democratic-Republican Party grew the Democratic Party—the party still claims Jefferson as one of their party founders and celebrates their beginnings as the party of Jefferson with a Jefferson-Jackson Day dinner fundraiser. The Democratic Party of Jackson introduced many mechanisms of party politics that are still in use today including party platforms used by the party to explain political positions on the issues of the day. During the late 1820s until the advent of the Civil War, the Democratic Party battled with the Whigs for control of the White House with the election of Andrew Jackson (1829-37), Martin Van Buren (1837-41), James Polk (1845-49), Franklin Pierce (1853-57), and James Buchanan (1857-61).

The Democratic-Republican Party was broken into pieces after the election of John Quincy Adams forming a National Republican Party which swallowed up the Whig Party which formed in the early 1830s. The Whig Party had an early success in presidential politics with the election of William Henry Harrison, who was the first candidate from the party to win the office. The Whigs by and large favored the power of Congress over the Presidency and took their name from the revolutionary Whigs who fought the king in 1776. There were actually 4 Whig presidents—William Henry Harrison (1841), John Tyler (1841-45), Zachary Taylor (1849-50), and Millard Fillmore (1850-53)—Tyler and Fillmore succeeded to the presidency upon the deaths of Harrison and Taylor. In the election of 1848, former Democratic President Martin Van Buren had been nominated by the Free-Soil Party. The party did not want new territories added to the Union unless they prohibited slavery. Enough Democrats peeled away from the Democratic candidate, that Whig Zachary Taylor was elected. However, the Whig Party dissolved not long after that and merged into the Republican Party in the 1850s.

In the 1850s the Republican Party was formed out of the remnants of the Whig Party and the Anti-Slavery Democrats of the North. The Republican Party was anti-slavery and was able to capitalize on the split of the Democratic Party on the issue grabbing the White House in 1860 and holding it from then until Woodrow Wilson was elected president in 1912, except for the two non-consecutive terms of Grover Cleveland in 1884 and 1892. Beginning with the election of Abraham Lincoln, the Republican Party captured the White House almost continuously from 1860 to 1912: Ulysses Grant (1869-77), Rutherford Hayes (1877-81), James Garfield (1881), Chester Arthur (1881-85), Benjamin Harrison (1889-93), William McKinley (1897-1901), Theodore Roosevelt (1901-09), and William Taft (1909-1913).

From the birth of the Republican Party in 1856 to the present day, the Democratic and Republican Parties have dominated American presidential politics. America, since the election of 1860, essentially became a two-party system. Only occasionally have third parties emerged to play an important role in our political system. In the election of 1912, the Republican Party was split in their vote between incumbent President William Howard Taft and third party candidate of the Bull Moose Party, Theodore Roosevelt who had been a Republican. The vote split and Woodrow Wilson won on the Democratic ticket.

Political Parties Review

1. Have all presidents belonged to a political party?

   _____

2. What four political parties have had candidates who have won the presidency?

   _____

3. What is the oldest political party in the United States?

   _____

4. How many presidents were there who belonged to the Whig Party?

   _____

5. What political Party was formed out of the Whig Party, the Free-soilers, and the abolitionists?

   _____

6. Who warned against the formation of political parties?

   _____

7. Who was the only person from the Federalist Party to serve as president?

   _____

Political Parties Handout: 1

German-born Thomas Nast (September 27, 1840 – December 7, 1902) was a famous political cartoonist. His drawings of Santa Claus and Uncle Sam were so famous they have become the images we think of when we think of the jolly and rotund Santa Claus or the thin and stars-and-striped bedecked Uncle Sam. He also created the symbols for the Republican and Democratic Parties—the elephant and the donkey, respectively. His career as a political cartoon spanned over three decades as was spent working for Frank Leslie's Illustrated Newspaper, New York Illustrated News, and Harper's Weekly, which is where he spent most of his career.

The political cartoon, STRANGER THINGS HAVE HAPPENED, was drawn by Thomas Nast, one of the first and best-known political cartoonists of the Nineteenth Century. Many historians consider him the father of the political cartoon. Nast was the cartoonist who developed the symbols for the two major political parties during his career as a cartoonist. In this cartoon, drawn in 1879 and published in the December 29, 1829 issue of Harper's Weekly, depict the Democratic donkey and the Republican elephant together in a cartoon for the first time.

In the cartoon, two United States politicians are shown next to their political symbols. The tall lean man with the top hat is Ohio Republican United States Secretary of the Treasury John Sherman, who served from 1877 until 1881. Delaware Democratic Senator Thomas Bayard is shown holding on to the tail of the donkey that is slipping into what Nast titled "FINANCIAL CHAOS" in his cartoon, drawn as an abyss.

In the background is the White House with a flag with the date 1880 emblazoned on it. Both men were contenders for the upcoming presidential election. The issue at the heart of the cartoon was the gold standard and whether or not legal tender in the United States should be backed by gold.

Bayard sponsored legislation in Congress supporting the return of the gold standard—one such bill known as the Legal Tender Resolution. Just behind Bayard are the words, "SAFE AND SOUND FINANCIAL ROAD". Sherman on the other hand favored the introduction of sliver money which was valued at the time at 83 cents on the dollar compared to gold-backed money. The symbol of the Republican Party, the elephant is slumbering next to a boulder that says, "LET – WELL ENOUGH ALONE".

STRANGER THINGS HAVE HAPPENED.
HOLD ON, AND YOU MAY WALK OVER THE SLUGGISH ANIMAL UP THERE YET.

Political Parties

STRANGER THINGS HAVE HAPPENED.

HOLD ON, AND YOU MAY WALK OVER THE SLUGGISH ANIMAL UP THERE YET.

Read the Political Parties Handout: 1 and study the political cartoon drawn by Thomas Nast on the Political Parties Handout: 2 and answer the following questions:

1. What is the significance of the White House in this cartoon?

_____

_____

_____

2. Which person in the cartoon is a Democrat? What evidence tells you this?

_____

_____

_____

3. Which person in this cartoon is the Republican? What evidence tells you that?

_____

_____

_____

4. Thomas Nast believed in one position over the other regarding currency being backed by gold—what is known as the gold standard. What, in this cartoon, gives the reader a hint at what Nast viewed as the better position on currency?

_____

_____

5. Both of these men were thought of as possible candidates for the United States presidency. Did either become president? Who did?

_____

_____

On the Campaign Trail

The campaign trail for any presidential candidate is an exciting time. There are speeches to make, debates to win, and babies to kiss! But the style of campaigning has changed over the course of the years and is vastly different from that of our forefathers. For example, in 1751, James Madison did not campaign for himself because doing so was considered undignified. The best way for him, and other presidential candidates of the day, was to have their supporters muster up rallies on their behalf, write pamphlets and letters to the newspapers.

The country was still small and limited transportation determined how a candidate might campaign. As the country and industry grew so did the way politicians sought out voters. In his 1896 campaign, William McKinley spoke to large crowds that were brought to his home in Canton, Ohio, and the term, "front porch" campaign came to be. By 1948, candidates crisscrossed the country by train to gain voters. From railway cars, the candidates gave speeches in what is known as "whistle-stop campaigns."

Today, once a nominee for president is announced at the national party convention, they work from Labor Day to Election Day to reach the voting public. Political advisors, attorneys, and accountants are hired to develop strategies on how to best get the word out. Speechwriters are hired to help the candidate clearly explain their party's platforms and goals to the public. Sometimes a candidate might promise to lower taxes, reduce unemployment or end the national debt. They might address international policies that include nuclear weapons, global warming, treaties, and the use of the United States military.

Candidates need to be great public speakers and surround themselves with knowledgeable historians, diplomats, economists, and strategists who share the same vision and give them sound advise. Candidates must also become extraordinary fundraisers because modern campaigns are longer, more complicated, and far more expensive than in the past.

Raising money on the campaign is critical to the candidate's success. Abraham Lincoln spent less than $700 to fund his campaign. The cost of a presidential race in 2012 was $2,621,415,792. The donated money is used to pay the staff, food, office rentals, travel expenses, mailing of postcards, handbills, and letters to voters. There are advertising campaigns in magazines, television and radio commercials, billboards, buttons bumper stickers, and even posters that are produced. It is important to remember that while there is so much money spent on campaigns, the United States is a big country. To reach its vast population costs a great deal of money in large markets.

It appears to be that the candidate who raises the most money has a better chance of winning the election. To create a more even 'playing field' in the world of elections, every so often new campaign reform laws are created to limit the amount of money that individuals or groups may give to a candidate. In the 1970s, people came to believe that raising so much money would lead to corruption due to graft so Congress passed reform bills that would change the face of campaign funding. These changes limited the amount of money that an individual or group could give to the candidates; they limited how much spending a candidate is allowed, but at the same time, they made money available from the federal government to finance campaigns. However, if presidential candidates were to take the money from the government they are not allowed to ask for private contributions.

Political Action Committees (PAC), are extremely important to campaigns. They came about as a result of the 1970 reforms in an effort to fund a campaign without breaking the law. A PAC is a type of large organization, such as a union, that pools contributions from its members and donates the funds to their candidate. The funds are limited if they are given directly to the candidates. However, PAC's are allowed to spend as much as they chose on their own independent campaigns that support the candidates.

A campaign cannot run without volunteers. These valuable people not only donate money but hundreds of hours of service by operating campaign headquarters, organizing town hall meetings, and parades in every state of the union for their candidates. Other volunteers canvass or go from door-to-door and to pass their candidates fliers out to the voters.

Campaigns are strategically planned in order to win. Each presidential candidate understands that they must gain the majority of seats in the Electoral College. They can do this in part by targeting different groups through endorsements by well-known actors or athletes; or, by using different types of media and sending information through the mail to niche voters, while appealing to a broader crowd over the television.

Sector	Description	Total Expenditures
Administrative	Travel & lodging	$68,173,185
	Rent, utilities & office expenses	$12,051,122
	Administrative data & technology	$9,421,141
	Accountants, compliance & legal services	$9,350,315
	Administrative consulting	$6,354,299
	Miscellaneous administrative	$2,682,596
	Administrative event expenses & food	$964,609
Campaign Expenses	Campaign mailings & materials	$25,974,843
	Campaign events & activities	$664,172
Contributions	Contributions to state & local parties	$110,282
	Miscellaneous contributions	$102,836
	Contributions to joint fundraising committees	$80,269
	Contributions to federal candidates	$73,632
	Contributions to committees	$39, 919
	Contributions to national parties	$2,400
	Contributions to state & local candidates	$1,000
Fundraising	Fundraising mailings & calls	$86,570,758
	Fundraising consulting	$52,495,929
	Fundraising fees	$22,063,986
	Fundraising events	$8,075,377
	Fundraising data & technology	$6,981,959
	Miscellaneous fundraising	$3,015,870

Used with permission from the Center for Responsive Politics (opensecrets.org)

Sector	Description	Total Expenditures
Media	Unspecified media buys	$594,690,686
	Web ads	$94,473,107
	Media consulting	$30,087,695
	Media production	$17,885,512
	Miscellaneous media	$15,438,098
	Broadcast ads	$8,548,406
	Print ads	$2,398,810
Salaries	Salaries & wages	$98,321,488
Strategy & Research	Campaign strategy amd communications consulting	$24,903,019
	Polling & surveys	$22,809,918
	Campaign data & technology	$484,338
	Transfers to state & local parties	$21,214,791
Transfers	Transfers to national parties	$8,717,480
	Transfers to committees	$444,687
	Transfers to candidates	$5,250
Unclassifiable	Unclassifiable event expenses	$25,812,350
	Unclassifiable printing & shipping	$13,550,694
	Unclassifiable consulting	$7,374,465
	Unclassifiable data & technology	$4,419,669
	Unclassifiable supplies & equipment	$818

You are the Campaign Manager and it is up to you to budget your candidate's finances. You are given $100,000 to work with. Review the spending on the chart on the previous page. Remember that much of a campaign's funds go to the media for advertising but there are also additional expenses that you need to consider. When you've completed your chart below, add up the expenditures to see if you are within budget. You will probably have to adjust some of the amounts to stay within your $100,000.00. When you adjust the amount, write down your thoughts on how and why you adjusted your spending.

Sector	Description	Total Expenditures
Administrative	Travel & lodging	
	Rent, utilities & office expenses	
	Accountants, compliance & legal services	
	Expenses & food	
Campaign Expenses	Campaign mailings & materials	
	Campaign events & activities	
Contributions	Contributions to state & local parties	
	Miscellaneous contributions	
	Contributions to committees	
	Contributions to national parties	
Fundraising	Fundraising mailings & calls	
	Fundraising consulting	
	Fundraising fees	
	Fundraising events	
	Fundraising data & technology	
	Miscellaneous fundraising	

Sector	Description	Total Expenditures
Media	Unspecified media buys	
	Web ads	
	Media consulting	
	Media production	
	Miscellaneous media	
	Broadcast ads	
	Print ads	
Salaries	Salaries & wages	
Strategy & Research	Campaign strategy & communications consulting	
	Campaign data & technology	
Unclassifiable	Unclassifiable event expenses	
	Unclassifiable printing & shipping	
	Unclassifiable consulting	
	Unclassifiable data & technology	
	Unclassifiable supplies & equipment	

Used with permission from the Center for Responsive Politics (opensecrets.org)

First in the Nation: The Iowa Caucus and the New Hampshire Primary

Words to look for

Caucus   Precinct   Primary   Delegates

States that use the caucus system are Alaska, Colorado, Hawaii, Kansas, Maine, Minnesota, Nevada, North Dakota, Wyoming and Iowa. Caucuses are different than primaries in that the voting is done very differently. There is no secret ballot. Instead people of each party at their precincts gather in groups dictated by the candidate to whom they pledge support.

What makes the Iowa caucus special is that it is the first caucus to take place during the presidential nominating election cycle. Since 1972, the Iowa caucus has been the first. Because it is the first political event in the nomination process for each political party reporters flock to the state to cover the outcome. Television coverage of the results makes big news. If a candidate comes out on top, they get a big bump. If a candidate comes in second or third, it can sometimes mean that they lose donors and momentum. So, the stakes are big for each of the candidates in the race for the Democratic and Republican nominating process.

Iowa is a large state in terms of square miles but has a relatively small population. The 99 counties in the state are divided into 1,774 precincts. Each of the precincts sends delegates to the county nominating convention, which in turn sends delegates to the state convention and finally the national nominating convention.

Following closely on the heels of the Iowa caucus, is the New Hampshire primary. Since 1920—it has been the first in the nation primary. As such, reporters flood into the state to follow the candidates on campaign stops and eventually to cover the results of the primary votes. Again, the stakes are high. The results of the primary can give a fledgling campaign a boost or cause it to stall.

Both Iowa and New Hampshire are small in population and many believe that their populations are not representative of the population of the United States at large. Some have advocated for other more populous states to take the lead in the nominating process but so far this has not happened.

The First in the Nation: The Iowa Caucus and the New Hampshire Primary

Read the questions below and answer them.

1. Explain what is caucus is.

_____

_____

_____

2. How is a caucus different than a primary?

_____

_____

_____

_____

3. When and where is the first caucus in the nominating process for a president held?

_____

_____

_____

_____

4. When and where is the first in the nation primary held?

_____

_____

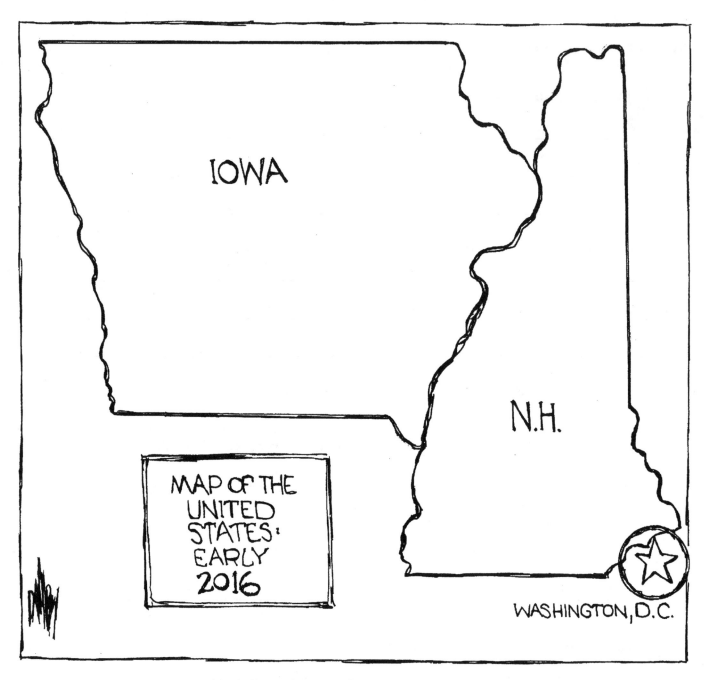

Used with permission from George Danby / Bangor News

Name _____

First in the Nation: The Iowa Caucus and the New Hampshire Primary

Study the political cartoon in First in the Nation: The Iowa Caucus and the New Hampshire Primary Handout: 1 and read and answer the question below.

1. Explain how a caucus is different than a primary.

_____

_____

_____

_____

2. In what state is the first-in-the nation caucus held?

_____

3. In what state is the first-in-the nation primary held?

_____

4. Look at the map in the political cartoon. Why does the map only display two states on the map of the United States?

_____

_____

_____

5. What statement is the political cartoonist making?

_____

_____

_____

_____

The Conventions

Words and phrases to look for

Convention   Delegated   Super delegate   Platform

Planks   Brokered convention   Horse trading

National conventions are huge political gatherings that are set up to determine who will represent the party during the presidential campaign. When presidential candidates go to the national conventions they have already spent a great deal of time campaigning against their opponents during the primaries and caucuses.

The national conventions are typically held in convention centers of major cities. Within the last few decades, these massive party get-togethers have favored stadiums to accommodate the increasing capacity.

Historically, the conventions were used for party debates and bargaining until one nominee rose to the 'top of the heap' and was chosen as their presidential candidate. Today conventions are also used to gain as much media attention as possible not only for their party and candidates but also for developing new platforms.

Around eighteen months before a national convention begins, a Call to Convention is issued. This is a formal invitation from the national party to members of each state and territory. While there are others, the two major conventions held are for the Democratic and Republican parties. Each political party establishes their own rules for participating in the nominating convention. These rules include, a number of voting representatives known as "delegates.'

The delegates are people chosen at the state level by each political party. Only party delegates are allowed to vote for presidential nominees. The amount of delegates for each state depends upon the population. During a convention, a party invites non-delegate officials and activists, Congressional Representatives, various guests, international observers, not to mention numerous members of the news media, volunteers, protesters, local business proprietors, and promoters hoping to capitalize on the event.

The nominees must receive a preset majority of votes from the delegates in order to become the party's presidential candidate. But the most important component to these closed contests are the "super delegates." Be it Democratic or Republican, a "super delegate" is a party leader or official who is free to support any party candidate. For the Democratic party there are around 800 unpledged party leaders and elected officials who are given super delegate status by virtue of the positions they hold rather than by the votes they cast in primaries and caucuses. Because of their numbers these super delegates carry a lot of clout.

The Rallies

Each day of the convention, party activists hold "rallies" or meetings to form a "platform." The platform is a statement of the party's principles, public policy goals and strategies that address important political issues. The party's platforms are broken down into statements or declarations known as "planks." Some of these planks appeal to special interest groups. Most important, party platforms and planks give candidates a clear political position which they will use to campaign. They also give voters an idea of what each candidate, if elected, will change once in office.

During the convention, party leaders make major speeches that address the party interests, direction and platforms. All voting for the new platforms and nominees is done in the evening. On the last day of the convention, the nominees for the president and vice president make their formal acceptance speeches.

Brokered Conventions

Before the presidential nomination begins, there is usually a front runner who has already emerged from the party. But if no single candidate receives a majority of votes by the delegates, then a 'brokered convention' is established. This is when a candidate is actually selected during the convention. A good example of this is during the 1976 Republican National Convention. Neither Gerald Ford nor Ronald Reagan received enough votes in the primaries to move forward.

Ford had actually won more primary delegates and popular votes than Reagan during the convention but he did not have enough to secure his nomination. During the convention both candidates could possibly win so the hard politicking and fun began. Both men openly wooed uncommitted delegates in an effort to secure their votes. Even their campaign staffs played a role in gaining the commitments from delegates. In real political nature, Reagan's team blamed Ford's administration for various actions against the Soviet Union and indirectly faulted him for the fall of Saigon in 1971. On the other hand, Ford's team gave special perks to super delegates, such as trips abroad on the president's private jet, Airforce One. After much manipulation and horse-trading Gerald Ford came out the victor during the Republican convention-but, he won it by a just a little over 100 votes.

How the delegates vote

Voting during the national conventions has changed little from when they first began. The voting method is called a "rolling roll call of the states" but the vote also includes the 16 territories of the United States. The states are called in alphabetical order. A spokesperson begins with a glowing speech about their state and notable party officials; then they announce their delegate vote as a count or a "pass". Some states pass on the first round. When all the states have voted, those who passed are called upon once more to announce their choice of presidential nominee.

Project: Looking at Platforms and Planks

Every four years, the political parties hold conventions that determine the direction of the party with newly elected presidential candidates and refined platforms with planks.

Platforms and planks are the set of goals, principles and strategies that address political issues. The party platforms are broken down into declarations (or planks) that address each specific issue.

Review the various Democratic and Republican platform comparisons from 2012. * Due to space limitations, only a select number of planks have been included.

	2012 Democratic Party Platform	2012 Republican Party Platform
Source Document	2012-National-Platform.pdf	2012 GOPPlatform.pdf
Foreign Policy: Foreign Aid	We will continue to respond to humanitarian crises around the globe.	Limiting foreign aid spending helps keep taxes lower, which frees more resources in the private and charitable sectors, whose giving tends to be more effective and efficient.
Commerce: Minimum Wage	We will raise the minimum wage, and index it to inflation.	
Commerce: Small Businesses	President Obama and the Democratic Party are committed to... tax cuts for small businesses that make new investments, hire more workers, or increase wages.	We will reform the tax code to allow businesses to generate enough capital to grow and create jobs...
Crime	We will continue to invest in proven community-based law enforcement programs such as the Community Oriented Policing Services program.... We created the Federal Interagency Reentry Council in 2011.... We support local prison-to-work programs....	We support mandatory prison sentencing for gang crimes, violent or sexual offenses against children, repeat drug dealers, rape, robbery and murder. We support a national registry for convicted child murderers. We oppose parole for dangerous or repeat felons.
	We enacted the Fair Sentencing Act....	In solidarity with those who protect us, we call for mandatory prison time for all assaults involving serious injury to law enforcement officers.

	2012 Democratic Party Platform	2012 Republican Party Platform
	We have increased funding for the Byrne Justice Assistance Grant Program over the last four years, and we will continue to expand the use of drug courts....	Federal criminal law should focus on acts by federal employees or acts committed on federal property – and leave the rest to the States. Then Congress should withdraw from federal departments and agencies the power to criminalize behavior....
Energy	President Obama has encouraged innovation to reach his goal of generating 80 percent of our electricity from clean energy sources by 2035. Democrats support making America the world's leader in building a clean energy economy by extending clean energy incentives.	We will end the EPA's war on coal.... Further, we oppose any and all cap and trade legislation.
	We support more infrastructure investment to speed the transition to cleaner fuels in the transportation sector.	We call for timely processing of new reactor applications currently pending at the Nuclear Regulatory Commission.
	Democrats will fight to cut tax subsidies for Big Oil while promoting job growth in the clean energy sector....	We will respect the States' proven ability to regulate the use of hydraulic fracturing, continue development of oil and gas resources in places like the Bakken formation and Marcellus Shale, and review the environmental laws that often thwart new energy exploration and production. We salute the Republican Members of the House of Representatives for passing the Domestic Energy and Jobs Act....
Environment	Harnessing our natural gas resources needs to be done in a safe and responsible manner, which is why the Obama administration has proposed a number of safeguards to protect against water contamination and air pollution. We will continue to advocate for the use of this clean fossil fuel, while ensuring that public and environmental health and workers' safety are protected.	As soon as possible, we will reverse the current Administration's blocking of the Keystone XL Pipeline....

	2012 Democratic Party Platform	2012 Republican Party Platform
Environment	Democrats are committed to balancing environmental protection with development, and that means preserving sensitive public lands from exploration, like the Arctic National Wildlife Refuge, Pacific West Coast, Gulf of Maine, and other irreplaceable national landscapes.	We support opening the Outer Continental Shelf (OCS) for energy exploration and development and ending the current Administration's moratorium on permitting; opening the coastal plain of the Arctic National Wildlife Refuge (ANWR) for exploration and production of oil and natural gas; and allowing for more oil and natural gas exploration on federally owned and controlled land.
Energy	Democrats will fight to cut tax subsidies for Big Oil while promoting job growth in the clean energy sector....	We stand with growers and producers in defense of their water rights against attempts by the EPA and the Army Corps of Engineers to expand jurisdiction over water....
Supreme Court	We will continue to nominate and confirm judges who are men and women of unquestionable talent and character and will always demonstrate their faithfulness to our law and our Constitution and bring with them a sense of how American society works and how the American people.	Public access to public lands for recreational activities such as hunting, fishing, and recreational shooting should be permitted on all appropriate federal lands. We support the appointment of judges who respect traditional family values and the sanctity of innocent human life.
Healthcare	We believe accessible, affordable, high quality health care is part of the American promise, that Americans should have the security that comes with good health care, and that no one should go broke because they get sick. We will continue to stand up to Republicans working to take away the benefits and protections that are already helping millions of Americans every day. We refuse to go back to the days when health insurance companies had unchecked power to cancel your health policy, deny you coverage, or charge women more than men.	

	2012 Democratic Party Platform	2012 Republican Party Platform
Housing	We Democrats support lowering the corporate tax rate while closing unnecessary loopholes, and lowering rates even further for manufacturers who create good jobs at home.	The FHA … must be downsized and limited to helping first-time homebuyers and low- and moderate income borrowers.
Immigration	We won't deport deserving young people who are Americans in every way but on paper, and we will work to make it possible for foreign students earning advanced degrees in science, technology, engineering, and mathematics to stay and help create jobs here at home. A policy of strategic immigration, granting more work visas to holders of advanced degrees in science, technology, engineering, and math.	The country urgently needs comprehensive immigration reform that brings undocumented immigrants out of the shadows and requires them to get right with the law, learn English, and pay taxes in order to get on a path to earn citizenship. Foreign students who graduate from an American university with an advanced degree… should be encouraged to remain here and contribute to economic prosperity and job creation. Highly skilled, English speaking, and integrated into their communities, they are too valuable a resource to lose. We support changing the way that the decennial census is conducted, so that citizens are distinguished from lawfully present aliens and illegal aliens. We oppose any form of amnesty….

[Reference Source: WHAT YOUR VOTE MEANS, IN THEIR OWN WORDS: A Side-by-Side Comparison of the 2012 Democratic and Republican Party Platform Documents http://crhofmann.com/2012/09/24/compare-the-democratic-and-republican-platforms-2/]

Name _____

The Conventions Review

Read and answer the questions below:

1. Review the above planks that make up the platforms. Pick one from each party (Democrat and Republican) and compare.

_____

_____

_____

_____

_____

2. Do you think that the party leaders today have remained faithful to their political platforms? Why or why not?

_____

_____

_____

_____

_____

3. Being a party member does not necessarily mean that you must agree with every plank in your party's platform. Based on what you have studied which party do you agree with? Why?

_____

_____

_____

_____

_____

The Vice-Presidential Pick

Each presidential candidate must pick their choice of vice-president to be their running mate during their party's national convention. The choice of vice-president could make, or break, the chances of winning the election.

The strengths of the vice-presidential candidate should "balance" the ticket or compensate for any weaknesses that the presidential candidate might have. It also makes a difference whether the vice-presidential candidate is capable of carrying an important state or region during the campaign so that they are able to gain as many votes as possible. This was the case with John F. Kennedy and vice-president, Lyndon B. Johnson. Both men were Democrats but from different regions of the country. John F. Kennedy was from Massachusetts and needed a good, solid running mate so he could win the Southern votes. He found this in Lyndon B. Johnson who was from Texas and had a long and impressive career as a senator.

Some vice-presidential candidates are chosen to help heal wounds in a party or reinforce the goals of the campaign. Such was the case with Abraham Lincoln's running mate, Andrew Johnson. In 1865, the Civil War was drawing to a close and Lincoln needed a Southerner to be on the same ticket in order to gain the trust of the southern states and hopefully help the country heal from the devastating war and restore the union.

The 2008 elections are a good example of strategic planning for choosing vice-presidential running mates. With hopes of gaining more votes, John McCain (Republican) chose his running mate, Sarah Palin, as a move to capture the social conservatives and appeal to the women voters. Whereas, Barrack Obama (Democrat), who had little experience in government, chose to offset this weakness by chosing Sentator Joseph Biden who had 26 years of experience in government.

Since the beginning, the office of the vice-president was considered minor and insignificant. John Adams was the first vice-president to George Washington and said, "My country has in its wisdom contrived for me the most insignificant office that ever the invention of man contrived or his imagination conceived." But the lack of responsibility changed in the 20th century when Vice President Thomas R. Marshall began to chair some of President Woodrow Wilson's cabinet meetings. By the 1950's, President Dwight D. Eisenhower allowed his Vice-President, Richard M. Nixon, to not only attend cabinet meetings but also very important national security councils.

Today, vice-presidents officially preside over presidential cabinet meetings and remain one of four members of the National Security Council. Vice-presidents also assume temporary control of the executive branch if a president suffers from illness, undergoes surgeries, or is hospitalized for any reason.

While the vice-president has limited responsibilities the position is important. Today the vice-president is considered the 'President of the Senate' and it is his or her vote that breaks any ties. In this way the vice-president can still influence the state of the nation. The office of the vice-president is considered a stepping-stone to the presidency. In the history of our country's government there have been five men who had been elected as president after their terms as vice-presidents were fulfilled. Eight vice-presidents automatically became presidents when the elected president died in office. Finally, one vice president, Gerald Ford, became president after the resignation of Richard M. Nixon.

Whomever the presidential candidate chooses as a running mate, the vice-presidential candidate must have the party's backing. In a way, the presidential and vice-presidential candidates are running mates in this long race and there are many considerations and important strategies that go into making the right partnership.

Project: Presidential Picks Crossword Puzzle

Write the correct word below then add the corrected to the puzzle.

Across

1. The strengths of the vice-presidential candidate should _____ the ticket or compensate for any weaknesses of the presidential candidate.

2. Elections are a good example of _____ planning for choosing vice-presidential running mates.

3. The Vice President is the president of the _____ .

4. The _____ is the joint listing of the presidential and vice-presidential candidates on the same ballot.

7. To _____ means to select a person for public office by voting.

Down

5. The vice presidential candidate is known as the running _____ during the campaign.

6. A _____ is someone who speaks or acts on behalf of a party during the party's national convention.

8. The vice president's _____ breaks any ties in the senate

9. A group of individuals who advise a president are called _____ .

Historic Campaigns

Two hundred years ago, our Founding Fathers tackled hard issues and with them came diverse opinions and a good amount of dissent. But campaigning for the presidency, in spite of how it might have looked, was always serious business.

The only straightforward election in U.S. history was the one that put George Washington into office. In the next election, the Federalist Party wanted John Adams to follow Washington; and, the Democratic–Republicans wanted Thomas Jefferson as the second president of the United States. Unlike today, both candidates were prohibited from campaigning publicly and as a result, their supporters fought vicious battles in the press. The mudslinging began by referring to Jefferson as a 'mean lowlife atheist'; and, Adams was referred to as the man who wanted to be 'king.' The false innuendos and slurs never ended. The ruthlessness of both campaigns destroyed the friendship between men who had once been close and had served together in the Continental Congress and as ambassadors abroad.

As luck would have it, the voting procedures that were in place made Adams the President of the United States; and, his political rival, Jefferson, as his Vice-President. It was the worst possible match. Jefferson kept his eye on the executive seat and then ran against Adams in the following election. The 1800 rematch remains the only time an incumbent president has run against his vice president.

To better his odds, Jefferson dug deep into his bag of dirty tricks and hired a "hatchet man" who was a controversial political journalist and pamphleteer named, James Callendar. In the press, Callendar continued to discredit Adams and declared that Adams was determined to make war with France while Jefferson would keep the nation at peace. Then Callendar attacked Adams' character and called him a "strange compound of ignorance and ferocity, of deceit and weakness."

Adams chose not to disgrace himself so publicly. Instead, he and the Federalist-controlled Congress exploited the rising conflict with France by passing four laws, known as The Alien and Sedition Acts of 1798. These reforms outlawed the "false, scandalous, and malicious attacks" against Congress and the president. Soon, Callendar was arrested and convicted under the Sedition Act. In the end, Adams was the victor in the game of dirty politics.

Historically, most of our early presidents were somewhat passive in their approach to campaigning while in office. In 1836, William Henry Harrison became the first presidential nominee to go on the campaign trail. Though he spoke mostly of his personal triumphs during his days in the military, he did play an active role in his election by developing campaign strategies to letter writing.

Another case regarding historic elections includes Theodore Roosevelt.

Term limits for the presidents had yet to be established and Theodore Roosevelt had already won two terms when he stated that he would not run again. This created a "lame duck" situation for him and the last year of his presidency became ineffective. Never the less, he wanted to run for the presidency again and at all costs.

Roosevelt had also ostracized his own party leader by not giving the perks such as political favors. They looked to destroy Roosevelt's political career by not allowing him to run as the Republican candidate. So, he started his own party!

Roosevelt called his party the 'Bull Moose' and he ran his campaign with the energy and power that has yet to be matched. Unfortunately, because of his desire to win, Roosevelt also split his old Republican party leaving it too weak to have any political clout and a Democrat won the race.

There are many 'firsts' in American presidential history but the most notable to date was the election of President Barack Obama. He was the first African American to be elected into the executive branch of the government.

Barack Obama's race to the presidency began in the 2008 election year. At that time, the two candidates, Barack Obama and Hilary Clinton, ran against each other as the Democratic presidential nominees. Both were hoping to become president and either one would have made history-Hillary Clinton as the first woman nominated as president, or Obama as the first African American president. From February through June, they battled each other in the primaries and caucuses. But Obama's platform of "hope" and "change"; his ability to appeal to new and younger voters, plus his strategic approach to campaigning out organized Clinton. By not over-looking the seventeen states and territories that chose their delegates through caucuses Obama was able to win fourteen of the seventeen and took the lead. And, Clinton withdrew from the race.

The race was not over yet. Obama's new running mate and vice-president selection, Joseph Biden, would have to face off the Republican candidate, John McCain and his running mate, Sarah Palin. McCain maintained a narrow advantage in the polls but Obama's team began to outspend McCain's in both advertising and grassroots organizing. The biggest blow to McCain came with his running mate, Sarah Palin. Her limited knowledge of national and international policies revealed that she was unqualified to help run the country.

Obama won the race for the White House for two terms. Whatever legacy he left behind while serving as president, he will always be known as the first African American to become president.

Project: Collect and Analyze Campaign Ephemera

A. A perfect time to collect and analyze campaign ephemera is during the primaries. By doing this you will gain an understanding of how campaign strategies are developed while using advertising, marketing and publicity.

Things to looks for: Buttons, fliers, bumper stickers. Write down how many commercials, bus benches and radio spots there are.

1. What is the slogan? How is it being used?

_____

_____

_____

2. What are the candidates saying? Is this a negative campaign? If so, why?

_____

_____

_____

3. Debates: Listen carefully to the catch phrases. These words are:

_____

_____

4. Styles of a Campaign

_____

_____

_____

_____

Name _____

B. Pick one president and study the campaign strategy that his or her group used to win the election.

1. Who is the President and when did he or she run?

_____

2. What was the slogan that was used for the campaign?

_____

3. How did the slogan work with the party platform?

_____

4. Depending upon the candidate, were there ads, radio, bill boards, postcards, and other media? Did they work well together or did they look different and sound different?

_____

_____

_____

5. Compare the above campaign with current campaigns.

_____

_____

_____

6. What would you have done differently?

_____

_____

_____

7. What are the similarities between historic campaigns and current ones?

_____

_____

_____

_____

Campaigning in the Television Age

Words and phrases to look for

Media   Town hall meetings   Demeanor

Political analyst   Junket   Unbiased   Catch phrases

Political media experts are hired to establish solid coverage to get the candidates message to the public. This is accomplished through the Internet, newspapers, radio, television, and so on. But some of the most important tools candidates use to reach the voter is through debates, interviews, and town hall meetings. A campaign's ability to get information out early increases the candidate's level of funding and even popular interest. To do this means having a strong media campaign with strategic television placement and endorsements from popular actors or athletes.

The first time a presidential candidate used the television for their campaign was in 1952. At the time, Dwight D. Eisenhower's presidential campaign ran forty commercials that were twenty seconds spots. The commercial spots were called, "Eisenhower Answers America." In them, he appeared to be an accessible leader and answered the questions of ordinary citizens. Eisenhower won the election with his running partner, Richard Nixon.

Advertising Campaigns

Television has become an integral part of the candidate's presidential campaign because it remains the best way to reach the largest number of voters. Millions of dollars are spent on glitzy 30 to 60 minute spots that highlight the candidate's platforms and their backgrounds. Oftentimes, the television ads highlight the differences between the candidates or hit 'below the belt' in negative campaigns designed to show that one candidate is better than the other. The best way to get the most exposure is to have their commercials air during highly viewed programs such as sport events. Most of the advertising budgets are spent during the last few weeks of the campaign. Strategy comes into play when TV commercial spots are viewed in key areas of the county where the campaign mangers believe their message will bring in more votes.

In 1964, Lyndon B. Johnson's presidential campaign was the first to develop negative TV ads with "the Daisy Girl". In this commercial a young girl picks the petals off of a daisy. As she counted the petals, a nuclear bomb exploded in the distance. The commercial ended with an appeal to vote for Johnson. This commercial was less than a minute long and only aired once but its message was so powerful that it resulted in a victory for Johnson.

Richard M. Nixon's campaigns in 1972 were the most negative and yet they helped him win the election against McGovern-who did not enlist the aid of negative attacks until the last week of the campaign.

Because of the expense of commercials, candidates try to create as many opportunities for free exposure as possible. Often, the candidates invite reporters on the campaign trails. This way, the reporters air stories on presidents at Town Hall meetings, county fairs, schools, and anywhere else that would create attention and interest. Presidents who are running for re-election also take full advantage of newsworthy opportunities.

Debates

Using the television for debates did not begin until 1960 when four historic television debates were scheduled between John F. Kennedy and Richard M. Nixon. Over 70 million viewers watched with anticipation. Both men were well prepared but the public leaned towards Kennedy, his youth and calm demeanor were reassuring. On the other hand, Nixon looked nervous and began to sweat under the hot lights. Nixon worked hard to secure his position in the following debates but he never caught up to the public's initial reactions to Kennedy.

When the presidential elections took place, Kennedy received just .2 percent more of the votes. Political analysts believe that this small margin of votes was lost to Nixon because of the televised debates.

Political reporters and journalists cover what each candidate says and does on their publicity junkets. They should be unbiased in their reporting in order to give the public the right message but this is not always the case. Therefore, the public must be aware and scrutinize all messages.

Electronic Media

As the Internet grows, information that is not normally tackled by the political reporters is available. Sometimes, a candidate's advertising budget, data, and personal life is exposed and it often casts a negative light on the campaign. Nevertheless, today's researchers also bring many layers of valuable information to the voters.

Websites and email lists have become crucial and integral parts to the campaigns but the traditional means of campaigning- ad campaigns, mail, telephone polling, and face-to-face attention remains just as important.

Project: Organizing a Political Debate

In-class debates do not just teach public speaking; they also develop critical thinking; research skills and organization

1. Pick a current proposition or topic to debate.

2. Divide students into four groups. Two groups take turns against each other in a debate while the other two sit as an audience.

3. Designate one group to be "for" the proposition or topic, and the second group to be "against."

4. Allow students time to research the proposition before the debate begins. Explain that it is best they also study both sides of the argument so that they are prepared when called upon. Being prepared about a subject helps in anticpipating an opponents stance on a topic.

5. The debate begins: Move the first two A and B teams to opposite sides of the room. The C and D teams are the audience and will also ask questions regarding the topics. Pick straws for which team to go first.

6. Teacher or designated student keeps time.

7. How it works: Team "A" begins with the first student who is given 30 seconds to 1 minute to present an argument. "Time" is called after a minute. Then, they must ask one prepared question to the first student on Team B.

7. Team B: Answers the question posed to them with an effort to convince the audience. They have 1 minute to respond before "Time" is called. They must ask their prepared question to the second student on Team A.

8. The play back and forth between the students on each team continues until every member has a chance to respond and ask their question. The last student will ask their question to the student who began the debate on the opposite team.

9. Audience participation: The audience may address either team with a question. Once everyone is satisfied, the audience votes on which team was more successful in preparedness, debating by answering questions, and the most convincing.

10. Teams A and B sit as the audience while teams C and D debate the same topics in the manner of the last group.

Opinion Polls

Words and phrases to look for

Elector　　　Electoral College　　　Plurality

Some believe that public opinion polls unfairly influence the outcome of the elections because those candidates who are ahead have a great chance of raising money. It appears that the candidate who is able to raise the most amount of money wins the race to the Presidency. Nevertheless, polls are based on a set of questions that are used to determine how people feel about the candidates. The results from these public opinion polls are used in many ways. They influence the candidates, their strategy, give an idea of their popularity; and, determine where their campaign funds are spent or where the campaign managers should adjust their spending. Polls also give the public an idea of the candidate's popularity.

In the late 1800's polling was conducted by journalists who would conduct informal "straw polls" of average citizens to gauge public opinion during elections. Conducting these polls could be as easy as a newspaperman sitting in a train depot and questioning people who walked by, then publishing the results the next day.

In the 1930s, a popular magazine conducted public opinion polls of its subscribers. The magazine failed to notice that most of their subscribers were wealthier citizens. More than likely they were also Republican voters. Because of this, the results of the magazine predicted a landslide with Republican Alf Landon winning over Franklin D. Roosevelt. The magazine's polls were off balance and their results were proven wrong and Roosevelt won the presidency.

The first scientific polls were also conducted in 1936 by the statistician, George Gallop. He was the first to use "statistical modeling" which accurately predicted Franklin D. Roosevelt's standings in the public. For the last 50 years, Gallop Polls were respected for their accuracy and dominated the political scene until the 1990's when almost every news organization developed their own polls.

While polls are important tools, they should not be relied opon. An example of the inaccuracy of polling happened during the 1948 Presidential elections. Most polls had predicted the victory of Thomas E. Dewey over Harry S Truman. The night of the election, many newspapers neglected to wait for the official voter count and printed, "Dewy Defeats Truman" as the headlines in their newspapers. Unfortunately, the newspapers were wrong and once the votes were counted, Harry S Truman was elected the 31st President of the United States.

Because of this huge mistake with opinion polls, professional polling organizations have developed better techniques to taking samples of public opinions. Some of these techniques include integrating psychology and sociological research with the computer. Professional pollsters have also learned to make their findings more specific but- they make it very clear that their finds do not predict the outcome of any election!

"Sampling" public opinion is about finding a small group that reflects that largest population. According to the "Theory of Probability", it is not necessary to interview 200 million people for a poll but a smaller percentage of a group will give an indication to the mindset of a larger population. However, sample groups do have to reach a certain size in order to be statistically accurate.

The more accurate election polls are based on over 100,000 people randomly interviewed. Generally, most national polls are conducted over the phone. Poll workers dial a random number then conduct an interview with those who respond. Most poll workers try to compile at least 1500 responses. Then, they compare their responses to larger populations in terms of gender, age and race. Analysts also consider the conditions in which the polls were given. How questions are posed could produce misleading answers and weaken the accuracy of the polls.

But, polls conducted by telephone or through the email generally tend to not be as reliable as personal interviews. This is largely due to the fact that the pollster is not likely able to control who participates.

Project: Create Your Own Public Opinion Poll

Public polls help you understand the general thought about an issue and/or a candidate during an election. Take an informal poll at school or in your neighborhood based on your own questions. This project will help you better understand how important polls are as a gauge of public opinion. Always conduct your polls with adult supervision.

Think about what questions you will ask. Base the questions on what the current political candidates are discussing. Write out the list of questions.

Step 1. Rules

1. Make sure you pose the questions you ask as multiple choice, with yes/no answers. This will make your poll easier to tabulate.

2. Keep the questions to your poll short and simple.

3. Be sure that your questions do not force any answers. They must be unbiased otherwise your results will be open to criticism.

4. Ask someone to check your questions before you begin. Is your poll clear and easy to understand?

5. Make as many copies of your poll as necessary so that you can mark the answers without any influence.

Step 2. Select the Population Samples

1. Determine who you will ask when you take a poll. Will the opinions represent everyone in your community? Or, will your poll represent a small segment of your community divided by age, gender, etc.?

2. You don't have to poll the entire population to get an idea of how people feel. To get a random sample of the population you could, for example, telephone every fifth person on a phone book page. The point is to take a poll that is random and without bias.

Step 3. Conducting your poll

1. Prepare a brief introduction. When you approach a person make sure to introduce yourself. Explain the purpose of your poll and always ask if the person wouldn't mind taking a few minutes to answer your questions.

2. Remember: People who take the time to answer your poll are doing you a favor so be polite.

3. Explain to anyone who is willing to take your poll that their answers will be anonymous and they do not have to tell you their name.

4. Try to be organized by making your poll easy to take.

5. Make sure that all the questions have been completed accurately.

6. Tabulate your answers by adding them up. What do your answers represent?

Ask yourself: How difficult was it to conduct your poll? Do you think that you wrote down all the answers properly? Do you think that someone other than you might write the wrong answers? Do you think that it is possible to find a representative sample of voters by how you approached the public ?

**United States Constitution,
Article II, Section 1, Clause 2**

Each State shall appoint, in such Manner as the Legislature thereof may direct, a Number of Electors, equal to the whole Number of Senators and Representatives to which the State may be entitled in the Congress: but no Senator or Representative, or Person holding an Office of Trust or Profit under the United States, shall be appointed an Elector.

**United States Constitution,
Article II, Section 1, Clause 4**

The Congress may determine the Time of choosing the Electors, and the Day on which they shall give their Votes; which Day shall be the same throughout the United States.

The term Electoral College does not appear in the United States Constitution, but it is described in two clauses of Article II, the second and the fourth. The Electoral College is a device that was built into the United States Constitution for the election of the president. Because the framers of the constitution were wary of the uneducated masses voting directly for the president and maybe getting it wrong, they built in what they considered to be a safeguard.

As laid out in Article II, Section 1, Clause 2, each state has the number of electors that corresponds to their congressional delegation. That is, for every member of the House of Representatives and every member of the Senate a state has they have a corresponding elector, and consequently a corresponding electoral vote. So, for instance, Montana has one member of the House of Representatives and two Senators, therefore, Montana has three electoral votes. Currently, there are 538 electoral votes counted in every presidential election—435, one for each member of Congress, plus 100 for each member of the Senate, which totals 535. But in 1961, the 23rd Amendment was adopted, granting the District of Columbia three electoral votes. So, the Electoral vote count is now 538. A total of 270 electoral votes are now needed to win the presidency.

Twenty-third Amendment

Section 1. The District constituting the seat of Government of the United States shall appoint in such manner as the Congress may direct:

A number of electors of President and Vice President equal to the whole number of Senators and Representatives in Congress to which the District would be entitled if it were a State, but in no event more than the least populous State; they shall be in addition to those appointed by the States, but they shall be considered, for the purposes of the election of President and Vice President, to be electors appointed by a State; and they shall meet in the District and perform such duties as provided by the twelfth article of amendment.

Section 2. The Congress shall have power to enforce this article by appropriate legislation.[2]

The candidate that wins the state with a popular vote wins ALL of the electoral votes in what is called a winner take all system. This is true in every state but Maine (since 1972) and Nebraska (since 1996) where a different method for allocating electoral votes is used. In these two states, one elector within each congressional district is selected based on the popular vote for the presidential candidate within that district. Then, the remaining two electors are selected by the statewide popular vote. So, for instance, Nebraska has three congressional districts and two U. S. Senators.

In the election of 1824, Andrew Jackson who was running against three other candidates for the presidency, not only won the most popular votes but also the most electoral votes. However, because Jackson did not have a majority of electoral votes, meaning more than 50%, he did not automatically win the presidency. The election went to the House of Representatives where the members of the House voted and the second highest vote getter and electoral vote getter, John Quincy Adams, garnered the most votes.

Andrew Jackson
Electoral Vote: 99
States carried: 7
Popular Vote: 151,271
Percentage: 41.3%

John Quincy Adams
Electoral Vote: 84
States Carried: 13
Popular Vote: 113,122
Percentage: 30.9%

William H. Crawford
Electoral Vote: 41
States carried: 4
Popular Vote: 40,856
Percentage: 11.2%

Henry Clay
Electoral Vote: 37
States carried: N/A
Popular Vote: 47,531
Percentage: 13.0%

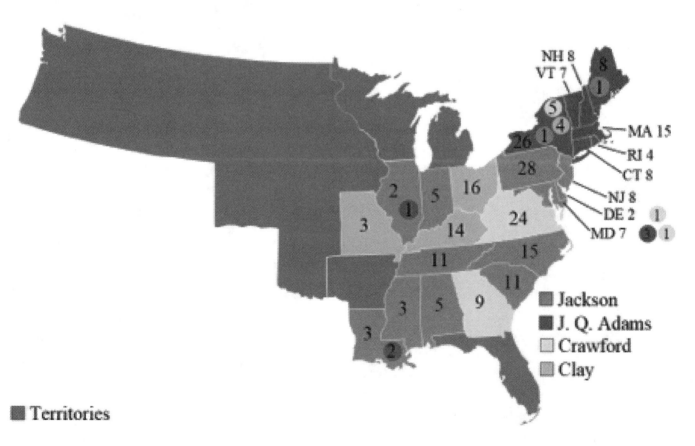

■ Territories

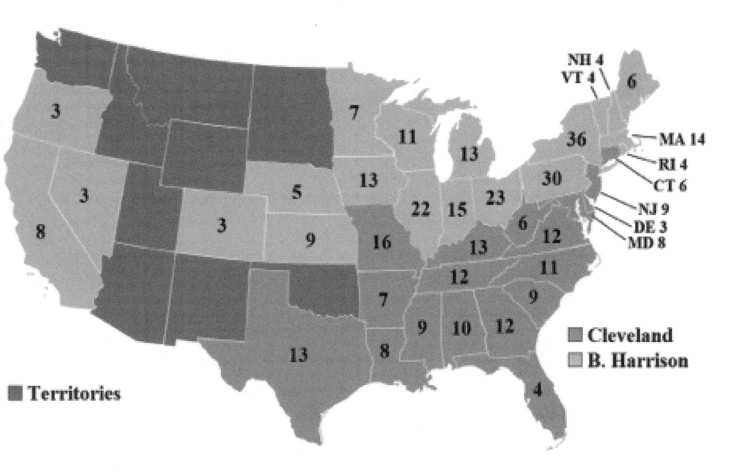

Three times in American history, the candidate who won the most electoral votes but did not win the popular vote, won the presidency:

In 1876, Rutherford Hayes defeated Samuel Tilden 185 to 184 in the Electoral College despite having 254,235 fewer popular votes.

The most recent case was in 2000 when George W. Bush defeated Al Gore 277 to 266 in the Electoral College despite George having over a half million fewer popular votes.

In 1888, Benjamin Harrison defeated Grover Cleveland 233 to 168 in the Electoral College despite having 90,596 fewer popular votes.

Election Day

In 1845, Congress passed a law that established the Tuesday after the first Monday of November as the official presidential election day. But why Tuesday? Lifestyles were different and Congress considered that the Sabbath was on Sunday. Farmers needed one full day to travel to the county seat to vote; and, Wednesday's were market days.

The first presidential elections were held in 1789. George Washington went to his home in Mount Vernon to await the election results. He had won the election unanimously by the use of the Electoral College instead of the popular vote. This system is still used today.

Nevertheless, today a tremendous amount of work, volunteers and money goes into the presidential elections and the final culmination of their efforts is revealed on Election Day. Candidates, their staff and volunteers worked tirelessly to get their message out. Everyone who is eligible and willing to vote sets out to their neighborhood precinct polling booths or mailed their secret ballots.

The voting process is carefully protected and privacy is insured. However, this was not always the case as in the late 1800's. At that time, voters yelled out their candidate's names. Later, colored ballots were used but others knew who was being voted on based on the color of the paper. In both cases, it was easy to threaten or bully citizens into voting for other candidates.

Today polling booths are areas approved by election officials. Some of the polling booths are at schools, town halls, and even garages. A voter's identity is checked from a list to insure that the person who comes is eligible to vote. A voter is given a ballot with all the names of the candidates. Then the voter steps inside a small booth and draws a curtain across to insure their privacy. Depending upon the precinct, a voter will either use a paper ballot, a lever machine with a punch card, or a computer.

When the last vote is turned in, the box is sealed by the election judge and transported to a central counting facility, such as a courthouse or city hall, and the votes are counted. Certified observers from the political parties watch to make sure that the counting is fair.

Paper ballots are read by two or more election officials to insure accuracy. Punch card ballots are counted manually and then run through a mechanical punch card reader. The software in the reader records the votes and prints out the totals. When the manual counts do not match the mechanical counts an election judge orders a recount. Problems arise when the cards stick together, the machine malfunctions or the cards are not fully punched. When this happens, the election judge will order all the ballots to be manually read. The punch card ballots became famous in the 2000 Presidential election because of the "hanging chads." No form of political campaigning is allowed at a voting place because the area is to remain clear of any influence by the various candidates, staff, and volunteers. Political buttons and posters are not even allowed. But campaign volunteers are able to do their last bit and help their candidates win by making phone calls to remind people to vote. Some drive the elderly to the polling precincts and do anything else to support their candidates in the final phase of the race.

The candidates also cast their votes at their precincts polling booths. Then they spend the rest of the day and evening with their supporters and watch the polls, political reporters and results on television. When Barrack Obama was a presidential candidate, he also enjoyed vigorous game of basketball with his friends to keep his mind off the presidential race.

The polling booths on the east coast close first. Slowly, polling booths in the central states close followed by the western states and Hawaii. Sometimes political analysts are able to tell if a candidate is winning but more often than not, the actual winner is unknown until all the votes from the polling booths, write-ins, mailed, and over-seas ballots are counted.

A candidate needs to win 270 Electoral College votes to win. When this happens, the losing candidates usually make a concession statement at their campaign headquarters. Television crews and reporters are there to catch the event. Once the statement is over, the television cameras switch to the victorious candidate's party headquarters and their victory statements are made to the public. The winning candidates and their staff celebrate their success after months of hard work.

Project: Voter Turnout-tabulating votes for the Candidates

During the next election you can follow the voter results in real time by watching the poll results on television, radio or the internet. Write-in the election results on map as the voting process happens. Use different colors for electoral votes.

*Note the numbers on the map are the electorial votes for each state.

Name _____

1. What are the voter qualifications in your state?

_____

2. How does a qualified person vote?

_____

3. Where is the closest voter precinct in your area?

_____

4. When is the next primary election? When is the next presidential election?

_____

Conducting a Voter Survey

Ask 18 to 20 people:

1. Are you registered to vote?

2. Are you registered as a Democrat, Republican or other?

3. Do you vote in every election?

Once you gather your answers ask how you can improve the voting process for the next time?

Notable Elections

Words and phrases to look for

Chads   Watergate   Notable Elections

I t's quite a feat to become president of the United States. George Washington is the only person to have been unanimously elected president and he remains a national hero today. Much of this has to do with the integrity of the man and the respect he had for the office. Nevertheless, in our political history, Franklin D. Roosevelt, came pretty close to being unanimously elected in 1936 with electoral votes at 523 to 8, as did Ronald Reagan in 1984 in which he won 523 votes over to 13. All three remain popular presidents today.

"Dewey Defeats Truman"

The 1948 presidential election campaign between Harry S. Truman and Thomas E. Dewey was a huge debacle. Never popular, Truman fought hard to gain votes and traveled thousands of miles, speaking out about the issues and what was wrong with the government. Truman eventually earned the slogan "Give 'em Hell, Harry!" because he was so aggressive with his campaigning but he also offered solutions to the problems. More and more people came out to listen to his speeches. His famous "whistle stop" campaigns drew the farmers and small town people out by the thousands. Truman's own party, the Democrats, didn't think he could win and threw very little money in his campaign.

Opinion polls taken at the time indicated that Dewey was the favorite by a huge lead. To keep this lead, his campaign staff insisted that Dewey avoid taking unnecessary risks and he never addressed the important issues.

On Election Day, the polls showed that Truman was gaining in the election race but Dewey remained the favorite lead. In anticipation of an easy win, newspaper editors began plugging early headlines that announced "Dewey Wins" in their newspapers before they knew the actual voting results. Political pundits wrote their early editorials and speculated on Dewey's presidency and his cabinet choices.

In the meantime, Truman and his family voted at their home precinct in Missouri and "Give 'em Hell" Harry went to bed early. The next morning he awoke to the news that he had won but the newspaper headlines were already printed and read, "DEWEY DEFEATS TRUMAN."

Watergate-The downfall of a President

While not notable in a good way, the worst election the country ever faced was with President Richard M. Nixon. But no one knew about his ruthlessness until after Nixon was reelected to his second term.

Nixon had been a popular president and he believed that he could win his term by simply doing his job. While he pretended that he did not have to campaign for his second term in 1972, privately he took the upcoming elections so seriously that he was willing to break the law. Nixon and a handful of his Republican inner-circle had the Democratic campaign headquarters at the Watergate Hotel in Washington, D.C., bugged and wired to listen in on conversations.

As the campaigns between the two parties progressed, Nixon's camp always remained a step ahead in its strategy, debates and polls and he won his second term. Nevertheless, Nixon and his team were eventually caught and he was forced to resign the presidency. The 'Watergate Scandal' impacted the way we view candidates and politicians today

Hanging, Dimpled and Pregnant Chads

The 2000 presidential campaign was one of the most hotly contested elections in contemporary times. The race was between Republican candidate, George W. Bush, and the Democratic candidate, Al Gore.

At the time, TV networks announced that Al Gore had won the crucial state. But that suddenly changed when the overseas ballots were counted and it looked as if Bush was the winner by a very slim margin. Florida law dictates that when the margins between two candidates are so close that there is an automatic ballot recount. For 36 days, the seat of the presidency was in limbo as each vote was manually recounted.

During the recount other problems arose. The state of Florida used paper ballots and Votomatic machines in their polling booths. The ballots had little windows with paper forms called "chads"that were punched out for each vote. Some of the ballots were disqualified when the chads hung from one or more corners ("hanging" chads); or, if the indentations had been made but the chads were still attached to the ballots and created "dimpled" or pregnant chads.

When ballot certifications showed that Bush lead the vote by a mere 537 votes, his legal team sought the U.S. Supreme Court to stop the recount efforts by citing that "the Constitution's guarantee of equal protection for all citizens disqualified a manual recount because Florida's counties had followed differing vote-counting procedures."

On December 12, the U.S. Supreme Court voted to stop the Florida recount. While Democrat, Al Gore, earned more popular votes than Bush, he conceded the next day and Bush won the presidency.

Name _____

Project

1. Who are the candidates running for the upcoming presidential and vice presidential elections today?

_____

_____

_____

2. Research their background using the Internet and their campaign websites.

3. Identify the names of the other smaller political parties and who is running as their candidates? Some of the parties might be, Green, Peace & Freedom, or Libertarian, and others.

_____

_____

_____

4. Primary Election Candidates

Presidential Candidates	Party	Conclusion

Vice Presidential Candidates	Party	Conclusion

5. Follow the primaries. Ask: Who has dropped out of the race and why? Who are the winners?

_____

_____

_____

_____

6. Who are the remaining Presidential Candidates and why?

Candidates	Party	Conclusion

Inauguration Day

Words and phrases to look for

Inauguration   President-elect   Fanfair

Over the years, the once simple ceremony created to swear in the President and Vice-President has turned into a large event with balls, parades and speeches. This day is called 'Inauguration Day.' The term of office for the President and Vice-president officially starts every four years on January 20th. This date was designated during President Franklin D. Roosevelt's second inauguration and it has remained that way ever since. Before the January 20th date there was a long, four month wait between the time that the newly elected president was inaugurated. This period was called the 'lame duck ' session because the outgoing president had little power or no influence with Congress; and, the incoming president was not yet legally in power. Our early forefathers used the 4 month gap to take care of personal business and then travel the long road to Washington, D.C. . The extended amount of time no longer made sense in the 1930's and the 20th Amendment closed the gap of time so that the government could run more efficiently.

Inauguration Day Activities

The important and spectacular Inauguration Day begins early with the President-elect participating in a morning worship session either by going to church, private service or attending an official prayer breakfast. After the morning worship service, the President-elect, Vice President-elect and their spouses, are escorted to the White House by members of the Joint Congressional Committee on Inaugural Ceremonies. The President-elect and the outgoing President have a brief meeting and together they proceed to the Capitol Building for the swearing-in ceremonies. The President and Vice-president stand on a massive platform with about 1600 people which include: Their families, members of House of Representative and U.S. Senate, cabinet members, justices of the Supreme Court, the outgoing president and vice-president, former presidents, governors, the joint chiefs of staff, and the diplomatic corps.

With all the special activities this important day brings the only thing that is mandated by the Constitution is the President's 'oath of office'. This oath, found in Article II, Section 1, must be said by noon. To do this, the incoming President or President-elect places his or her hand on the customary Bible or another form of Sacred text, and states: "I do solemnly swear [or affirm] that I will faithfully execute the Office of President of the United States, and will to the best of my ability, preserve, protect and defend the Constitution of the United States." If Inauguration Day falls on a Sunday, the Chief Justice administers the oaths to the incoming President and Vice-president during a private ceremony and the public oath and ceremonies are held on the following Monday.

Since 1981, the swearing-in ceremony has been held on west front side of the Capitol building. Once the President and Vice-president have been sworn in before the crowd, four 'ruffles and flourishes' are performed by the United States Marine Band. These ruffles (drums) and flourishes (bugles) are part of the elaborate fan-fair and are considered a tribute with the highest honors for the most celebrated people.

Then, the President's anthem, "Hail to the Chief" and the Vice-president's "Hail, Columbia" are played while a 21-gun salute is simultaneously fired by the Presidential Guns Salute Battery. This tradition dates as far back as the year 1818 when the 21 guns were meant to equal the number of states that were in the union. It is not mandatory, but some Presidents give an Inauguration Address to the public.

After the ceremony, the President and Vice-president are escorted to Statuary Hall in the Capitol Building for the traditional Inaugural Luncheon. This extravagant luncheon is hosted by the Joint Congressional Committee on Inaugural Ceremonies. All of the Congress and newly elected officials are invited. During the luncheon the President and Vice- President are presented with gifts given to them by the Congress on behalf of the American people.

Later, the new President and his entourage walk down Pennsylvania Avenue from the Capitol Building to the White House. If a new President takes over the executive office, due to the resignation or death of a president, the oath of office is given but the public events do not take place.

It is customary for the presidential entourage, including leading members of the government and military to watch the Inaugural Parade from the edge of the North lawn of the White House. The parade features the military and participants from all 50 states.

For the rest of the day and into the evening, festivities continue with balls and dinners. The Presidential Inaugural Balls are large official formal dances that celebrate the new presidential term. The President, Vice-president and their spouses make personal appearances at each ball held in their honor.

Name _____

Project

1. What day and time are the newly elected President and Vice-President sworn into office?

_____

2. What are 'Ruffles and Flourishes"?

_____

3. What happens when the Inauguration Day falls on a Sunday?

_____

4. Who administers the Oath of Office to the President and Vice-President?

_____

5. What is the title of the song played for Presidents when they are sworn in?

_____

6. What is the title of the song played for the Vice-Presidents when they are sworn in?

_____

7. What tradition to Inauguration Day dates back to 1812?

_____

8. When is a President sworn in but does not have a ceremony?

_____

9. What is the only tradition to Inauguration Day that is mandated by the Constitution?

_____

Appendix

 The Elections

The Election of 1789

Nominee: Washington
Electoral Vote: 69
States Carried: 8

Opponent: John Adams
Home state: Massachusetts
Electoral Vote: 34
States carried: 2

The Election of 1792

Nominee: Washington
Electoral Vote: 132
States Carried: 15
Popular Vote: 13,332

Opponent: John Adams
Home state: Massachusetts
Electoral Vote: 77
States carried:

The Election of 1796

Nominee: John Adams
Home State: Massachusetts
Running Mate: Thomas
Pinckney
Electoral Vote: 71
States Carried: 9
Popular Vote: 35,726
Percentage: 53.4%

Opponent: Thomas Jefferson
Home state: Virginia
Running Mate: Aaron Burr
Electoral Vote: 68
States carried: 7
Popular Vote: 31,115
Percentage: 46.6%

The Election of 1800

Nominee: Thomas Jefferson
Home State: Virginia
Running Mate: Aaron Burr
Electoral Vote: 73
States Carried: 8
Popular Vote: 41,330
Percentage: 61.4%

Opponent: John Adams
Home state: Massachusetts
Running Mate: Charles
Cotesworth Pinckney
Electoral Vote: 65
States carried: 7
Popular Vote: 25,952
Percentage: 38.6%

The Election of 1804

Nominee: Thomas Jefferson
Home State: Virginia
Running Mate: George
Clinton
Electoral Vote: 162
States Carried: 15
Popular Vote: 104,110
Percentage: 72.8%

Opponent: Charles
Cotesworth Pinckney
Home state: South Carolina
Party: Federalist
Running Mate: Rufus Kind
Electoral Vote: 14
States carried: 2
Popular Vote: 38,919
Percentage: 27.2%

The Election of 1808

Nominee: James Madison
Home State: Virginia
Running Mate: George
Clinton, John Langdon
Electoral Vote: 122
States Carried: 12
Popular Vote: 124,732
Percentage: 64.7%

Opponent: Charles
Cotesworth Pinckney
Home state: South Carolina
Party: Federalist
Running Mate: Rufus King
Electoral Vote: 47
States carried: 5
Popular Vote: 62,431
Percentage: 32.4%

The Election of 1812

Nominee: James Madison
Home State: Virginia
Party: Democratic-
Republican
Running Mate: Elbridge
Gerry
Electoral Vote: 128
States Carried: 11
Popular Vote: 140,431
Percentage: 50.4%

Opponent: DeWitt Clinton
Home state: New York
Party: Federalist
Running Mate: Jared
Ingersoll
Electoral Vote: 89
States carried: 7
Popular Vote: 132,781
Percentage: 47.6%

The Election of 1816

Nominee: James Monroe
Home State: Virginia
Party: Democratic-Republican
Running Mate: Daniel D. Tompkins
Electoral Vote: 183
States Carried: 16
Popular Vote: 76,593
Percentage: 68.2%

Opponent: Rufus King
Home state: New York
Party: Federalist
Running Mates: John Eager Howard, James Ross, John Marshall, Robert Goodloe Harper
Electoral Vote: 34
States carried: 3
Popular Vote: 34,740
Percentage: 30.9%

The Election of 1820

Nominee: James Monroe
Home State: Virginia
Party: Democratic-Republicans
Running Mates: Daniel D. Tompkins, Richard Stockton, Daniel Rodney, Robert Goodloe Harper
Electoral Vote: 228/231
States Carried: 23
Popular Vote: 87,343
Percentage: 80.6%

Opponent: John Quincy Adams
Home state: Massachusetts
Running Mate: Richard Rush
Electoral Vote: 1
States carried: 0
Popular Vote: N/A
Percentage: N/A

The Election of 1824

Nominee: John Quincy Adams
Home State: Massachusetts
Running Mate: John C. Calhoun, Andrew Jackson, Nathan Sanford, Henry Clay
Electoral Vote: 84
States Carried: 13 (after vote in the House of Represntatives)
Popular Vote: 113,122
Percentage: 30.9%

Opponent: Andrew Jackson
Home state: Tennessee
Party: Democratic-Republican
Running Mate: John C. Calhoun, Nathan Sanford
Electoral Vote: 99
States carried: 7 (after the vote in the House of Representatives)
Popular Vote: 151,271
Percentage: 41.3%

Opponent: William H. Crawford
Home state: Georgia
Party: Democratic-Republican
Running Mate: Nathaniel Macon, Martin Van Buren, Henry Clay, Nathan Sanford, Andrew Jackson
Electoral Vote: 41
States carried: 4 (after the vote in the House of Representatives)
Popular Vote: 40,856
Percentage: 11.2%

Opponent: Henry Clay
Home state: Kentucky

Party: Democratic-Republican
Running Mate: John C. Calhoun, Nathan Sanford, Andrew Jackson
Electoral Vote: 37
States carried: N/A
Popular Vote: 47,531
Percentage: 13.0%

The Election of 1828

Nominee: Andrew Jackson
Home State: Tennessee
Party: Democratic
Running Mate: John C. Calhoun, William Smith
Electoral Vote: 178
States Carried: 16
Popular Vote: 642,553
Percentage: 56.0%

Opponent: John Quincy Adams
Home state: Massachusetts
Party: National Republican
Running Mate: Richard Rush
Electoral Vote: 83
States carried: 10
Popular Vote: 500,897
Percentage: 43.6%

The Election of 1832

Nominee: Andrew Jackson
Home State: Tennessee
Party: Democratic
Running Mate: Martin Van Buren, William William
Electoral Vote: 219
States Carried: 16
Popular Vote: 701,780
Percentage: 54.2%

Opponent: Henry Clay
Home state: Kentucky
Party: National Republican
Running Mate: John Sergeant

Electoral Vote: 49
States carried: 6
Popular Vote: 484,205
Percentage: 37.4%

Opponent: John Floyd
Home state: Virginia
Party: Nullifier
Running Mate: Henry Lee
Electoral Vote: 11
States carried: 1
Popular Vote:
Percentage:

Opponent: William Wirt
Home state: Maryland
Party: Anti-Masonic
Running Mate: Amos Ellmaker
Electoral Vote: 7
States carried: 1
Popular Vote: 100,715
Percentage:7.8%

The Election of 1836

Nominee: Martin Van Buren
Home State: New York
Party: Democratic
Running Mate: Richard Mentor Johnson, William Smith
Electoral Vote: 170
States Carried: 15
Popular Vote: 764,176
Percentage: 50.8%

Opponent: William Henry Harrison
Home state: Ohio
Party: Whig Party - West
Running Mate: Francis P. Granger, John Tyler
Electoral Vote: 73
States carried: 7

Popular Vote: 550,816
Percentage: 36.6%

Opponent: Hugh Lawson White
Home state: Tennessee
Party: Whig Party - South
Running Mate: John Tyler
Electoral Vote: 26
States carried: 2
Popular Vote: 146,107
Percentage: 9.7%

Opponent: Daniel Webster
Home state: Massachusetts
Party: Whig Party – New England
Running Mate: Francis P. Granger
Electoral Vote: 14
States carried: 1
Popular Vote: 41.201
Percentage: 2.7%

Opponent: Willie Person Mangum
Home state: North Carolina
Party: Whig Party – South Carolina
Running Mate: John Tyler
Electoral Vote: 11
States carried: 1
Popular Vote: 0
Percentage: 0

The Election of 1840

Nominee: William Henry Harrison
Home State: Ohio
Party: Whig
Running Mate: John Tyler
Electoral Vote: 234
States Carried: 19
Popular Vote: 1,275,390
Percentage: 52.9%

Opponent: Martin Van Buren
Home state: New York
Party: Democratic
Running Mate: Richard Mentor Johnson, Littleton W. Tazewell, James Knox Polk
Electoral Vote: 60
States carried: 7
Popular Vote: 1,128,854
Percentage: 46.8%

The Election of 1844

Nominee: James Knox Polk
Home State: Tennessee
Party: Democratic
Running Mate: George M. Dallas
Electoral Vote: 170
States Carried: 15
Popular Vote: 1,339,494
Percentage: 49.5%

Opponent: Henry Clay
Home state: Kentucky
Party: Whig
Running Mate: Theodore Frelinghuysen
Electoral Vote: 105
States carried: 11
Popular Vote: 1,300,004
Percentage: 48.1%

The Election of 1848

Nominee: Zachary Taylor
Home State: Louisiana
Party: Whig
Running Mate: Millard Fillmore
Electoral Vote: 163
States Carried: 15
Popular Vote: 1,361,393
Percentage: 47.3%

Opponent: Lewis Cass
Home state: Michigan
Party: Democratic
Running Mate: William Orlando Butler
Electoral Vote: 127
States carried: 15
Popular Vote: 1,223,460
Percentage: 42.5%

The Election of 1852

Nominee: Franklin Pierce
Home State: New Hampshire
Party: Democratic
Running Mate: William R. King
Electoral Vote: 254
States Carried: 27
Popular Vote: 1,607.510
Percentage: 50.8%

Opponent: Winfield Scott
Home state: New Jersey
Party: Whig
Running Mate: William Alexander Graham
Electoral Vote: 42
States carried: 4
Popular Vote: 1,386,942
Percentage: 43.9%

The Election of 1856

Nominee: James Buchanan
Home State: Pennsylvania
Party: Democratic
Running Mate: John C. Breckinridge
Electoral Vote: 174
States Carried: 19
Popular Vote: 1,836,072
Percentage: 45.3%

Opponent: John C. Fremont
Home state: California

Party: Republican
Running Mate: William L. Dayton
Electoral Vote: 114
States carried: 11
Popular Vote: 1,342,345
Percentage: 33.1%
Opponent: Millard Fillmore
Home state: New York
Party: Know Nothing
Running Mate: Andrew Jackson Donelson
Electoral Vote: 8
States carried: 1
Popular Vote: 873,053
Percentage: 21.6%

The Election of 1860

Nominee: Abraham Lincoln
Home State: Illinois
Party: Republican
Running Mate: Hannibal Hamlin
Electoral Vote: 180
States Carried: 18
Popular Vote: 1,865,908
Percentage: 39.8%

Opponent: John C. Breckinridge
Home state: Kentucky
Party: Southern Democrat
Running Mate: Joseph Lane
Electoral Vote: 72
States carried: 11
Popular Vote: 848,019
Percentage: 18.1%

Opponent: John Bell
Home state: Tennessee
Party: Constitutional Union
Running Mate: Edward Everett
Electoral Vote: 39

States carried: 3
Popular Vote: 590,901
Percentage: 12.6%

Opponent: Stephen A. Douglas
Home state: Illinois
Party: Northern Democrat
Running Mate: Herschel Vespasian Johnson
Electoral Vote: 12
States carried: 1
Popular Vote: 1,380,202
Percentage: 29.5%

The Election of 1864

Nominee: Abraham Lincoln
Home State: Illinois
Party: Republican/National Union Party
Running Mate: Andrew Johnson
Electoral Vote: 212
States Carried: 22
Popular Vote: 2,218,388
Percentage: 55.0%

Opponent: George B. McCellan
Home state: Pennsylvania
Party: Democratic
Running Mate: George Hunt Pendleton
Electoral Vote: 21
States carried: 3
Popular Vote: 1,812,807
Percentage: 45.0%

The Election of 1868

Nominee: Ulysses S. Grant
Home State: Ohio
Running Mate: Schuyler Colfax
Electoral Vote: 214
States Carried: 26
Popular Vote: 3,013,650
Percentage: 52.7%

Opponent: Horatio Seymour
Home state: New York
Party: Democratic
Running Mate: Francis Preston Blair, Jr.
Electoral Vote: 80
States carried: 8
Popular Vote: 2,708,744
Percentage: 47.3%

The Election of 1872

Nominee: Ulysses S. Grant
Home State: Illinois
Party: Republican
Running Mate: Henry Wilson
Electoral Vote: 286
States Carried: 31
Popular Vote: 3,598,235
Percentage: 55.6%

Opponent: Horace Greeley
Home state: New York
Party: Liberal Republican
Running Mate: Benjamin Gratz Brown
Electoral Vote: 3/66
States carried: 6
Popular Vote: 2,834,761
Percentage: 43.8%

The Election of 1876

Nominee: Rutherford B. Hayes
Home State: Ohio
Party: Republican
Running Mate: William Almon Wheeler
Electoral Vote: 185
States Carried: 21
Popular Vote: 4,034,311
Percentage: 47.9%

Opponent: Samuel J. Tilden
Home state: New York
Party: Democratic
Running Mate: Thomas Andrews Hendricks
Electoral Vote: 184
States carried: 17
Popular Vote: 4,288,546
Percentage: 51.0%

The Election of 1880

Nominee: James Abram Garfield
Home State: Ohio
Party: Republican
Running Mate: Chester Alan Arthur
Electoral Vote: 214
States Carried: 19
Popular Vote: 4,446,158
Percentage: 48.3%

Opponent: Winfield Scott Hancock
Home state: Pennsylvania
Party: Democratic
Running Mate: William Hayden English
Electoral Vote: 155
States carried: 19
Popular Vote: 4,444,260
Percentage: 48.2%

The Election of 1884

Nominee: Grover Cleveland
Home State: New York
Party: Democratic
Running Mate: Thomas Andrews Hendricks
Electoral Vote: 219
States Carried: 20
Popular Vote: 4,874,621
Percentage: 48.5%

Opponent: James G. Blaine
Home state: Maine
Party: Republican
Running Mate: John Alexander Logan
Electoral Vote: 182
States carried: 17
Popular Vote: 4,848,936
Percentage: 48.2%

The Election of 1888

Nominee: Benjamin Harrison
Home State: Indiana
Party: Republican
Running Mate: Levi Parsons Morton
Electoral Vote: 233
States Carried: 19
Popular Vote: 5,443,892
Percentage: 47.8%

Opponent: Grover Cleveland
Home state: New York
Party: Democratic
Running Mate: Allen Granberry Thurman
Electoral Vote: 168
States carried: 17
Popular Vote: 5,534,488
Percentage: 48.6%

The Election of 1892

Nominee: Grover Cleveland
Home State: New York
Party: Democratic
Running Mate: Adlai E.
Stevenson I
Electoral Vote: 277
States Carried: 23
Popular Vote: 5,556,918
Percentage: 46.0%

Opponent: Benjamin
Harrison
Home state: Indiana
Party: Republican
Running Mate: Whitelaw
Reid
Electoral Vote: 145
States carried: 16
Popular Vote: 5,176,108
Percentage: 43.0%

Opponent: James Weaver
Home state: Iowa
Party: Populist
Running Mate: James Gaven
Field
Electoral Vote: 22
States carried: 5
Popular Vote: 1,041,028
Percentage:8.5%

The Election of 1896

Nominee: William McKinley
Home State: Ohio
Party: Republican
Running Mate: Garret
Augustus Hobart
Electoral Vote: 271
States Carried: 23
Popular Vote: 7,112,138
Percentage: 51.0%
Opponent: William Jennings
Bryan

Home state: Nebraska
Party: Democratic
Running Mate: Arthur Sewall,
Thomas Edward Watson
Electoral Vote: 176
States carried: 22
Popular Vote: 6,508,172
Percentage: 46.7%

The Election of 1900

Nominee: William McKinley
Home State: Ohio
Party: Republican
Running Mate: Theodore
Roosevelt
Electoral Vote: 292
States Carried: 28
Popular Vote: 7,228,864
Percentage: 51.6%

Opponent: William Jennings
Bryan
Home state: Nebraska
Party: Democratic
Running Mate: Adlai Ewing
Stevenson
Electoral Vote: 155
States carried: 17
Popular Vote: 6,370,932
Percentage: 45.5%

The Election of 1904

Nominee: Theodore
Roosevelt
Home State: New York
Party: Republican
Running Mate: Charles
Warren Fairbanks
Electoral Vote: 336
States Carried: 32
Popular Vote: 7,630,457
Percentage: 56.4%

Opponent: Alton Brooks
Parker
Home state: New York
Party: Democratic
Running Mate: Henry
Gassaway Davis
Electoral Vote: 140
States carried: 13
Popular Vote: 5,083,880
Percentage:

The Election of 1908

Nominee: William Howard
Taft
Home State: Ohio
Party: Republican
Running Mate: James S.
Sherman
Electoral Vote: 321
States Carried: 29
Popular Vote: 7,678,395
Percentage: 51.6%

Opponent: William Jennings
Bryan
Home state: Nebraska
Party: Democratic
Running Mate: John Worth
Kern
Electoral Vote: 162
States carried: 17
Popular Vote: 6,408,984
Percentage: 43.0%

The Election of 1912

Nominee: Woodrow Wilson
Home State: New Jersey
Party: Democratic
Running Mate: Thomas R.
Marshall
Electoral Vote: 435
States Carried: 40
Popular Vote: 6,296,284
Percentage: 41.8%

Opponent: Theodore
Roosevelt
Home state: New York
Party: Progressive
(Bull Moose)
Running Mate: Hiram
Johnson
Electoral Vote: 88
States carried: 6
Popular Vote: 4,122,721
Percentage: 27.4%

Opponent: William Howard
Taft
Home state: Ohio
Party: Republican
Running Mate: Nicholas
Murray Butler
Electoral Vote: 8
States carried: 2
Popular Vote: 3,486.242
Percentage: 23.2%

The Election of 1916

Nominee: Woodrow Wilson
Home State: New Jersey
Party: Democratic
Running Mate: Thomas Riley
Marshall
Electoral Vote: 277
States Carried: 30
Popular Vote: 9,126,868
Percentage: 49.2%
Opponent: Charles Evans
Hughes
Home state: New York
Party: Republican
Running Mate: Charles
Fairbanks
Electoral Vote: 254
States carried: 18
Popular Vote: 8,548,728
Percentage: 46.1%

The Election of 1920

Nominee: Warren G. Harding
Home State: Ohio
Party: Republican
Running Mate: Calvin
Coolidge
Electoral Vote: 404
States Carried: 37
Popular Vote: 16,144,093
Percentage: 60.3%

Opponent: James M. Cox
Home state: Ohio
Party: Democratic
Running Mate: Franklin
Delano Roosevelt
Electoral Vote: 127
States carried: 11
Popular Vote: 9,139,661
Percentage: 34.1%

The Election of 1924

Nominee: Calvin Coolidge
Home State: Massachusetts
Party: Republican
Running Mate: Charles G.
Dawes
Electoral Vote: 382
States Carried: 35
Popular Vote: 15,723,789
Percentage: 54.0%
Opponent: John W. Davis
Home state: West Virginia
Party: Democratic
Running Mate: Charles W.
Bryan
Electoral Vote: 136
States carried: 12
Popular Vote: 8,386.242
Percentage: 28.8%

Opponent: Robert M. La
Follette, Sr.
Home state: Wisconsin
Party: Progressive
Running Mate: Burton K.
Wheeler
Electoral Vote: 13
States carried: 1
Popular Vote: 4,831,706
Percentage: 16.6%

The Election of 1928

Nominee: Herbert Clark
Hoover
Home State: California
Party: Republican
Running Mate: Charles
Curtis
Electoral Vote: 444
States Carried: 40
Popular Vote: 21,427, 123
Percentage: 58.2%

Opponent: Al Smith
Home state: New York
Party: Democratic
Running Mate: Joseph Taylor
Robinson
Electoral Vote: 87
States carried: 8
Popular Vote: 15,015,464
Percentage: 40.8%

Nominee: Franklin D.
Roosevelt
Home State: New York
Party: Democratic
Running Mate: John Nance
Garner
Electoral Vote: 472
States Carried: 42
Popular Vote: 22,821,277
Percentage: 57.4%

Opponent: Herbert Hoover
Home state: California
Party: Republican
Running Mate: Charles Curtis
Electoral Vote: 59
States carried: 6
Popular Vote: 15,761,254
Percentage: 39.7%

The Election of 1932

Nominee: Franklin Delano Roosevelt
Home State: New York
Party: Democratic
Running Mate: John Nance Garner
Electoral Vote: 523
States Carried: 46
Popular Vote: 27,752648
Percentage: 60.8%

Opponent: Alf Landon
Home state: Kansas
Party: Republican
Running Mate: Frank Knox
Electoral Vote: 8
States carried: 2
Popular Vote: 16,681,862
Percentage: 36.5%

The Election of 1936

Nominee: Franklin Delano Roosevelt
Home State: New York
Party: Democratic
Running Mate: Henry A. Wallace
Electoral Vote: 449
States Carried: 38
Popular Vote: 27,313,945
Percentage: 54.7%

Opponent: Wendell Willkie
Home state: New York
Party: Republican
Running Mate: Charles L. McNary
Electoral Vote: 82
States carried: 10
Popular Vote: 22,347,744
Percentage: 44.8%

The Election of 1940

Nominee: Franklin Delano Roosevelt
Home State: New York
Party: Democratic
Running Mate: Harry S. Truman
Electoral Vote: 432
States Carried: 36
Popular Vote: 25,612,916
Percentage: 53.4%

Opponent: Thomas E. Dewey
Home state: New York
Party: Republican
Running Mate: John W. Bricker
Electoral Vote: 99
States carried: 12
Popular Vote: 22,017,929
Percentage: 45.9%

The Election of 1944

Nominee: Harry S Truman
Home State: Missouri
Party: Democratic
Running Mate: Alben W. Barkley
Electoral Vote: 303
States Carried: 28
Popular Vote: 24,179,347
Percentage: 49.6%

Opponent: Thomas E. Dewey
Home state: New York
Party: Republican
Running Mate: Earl Warren
Electoral Vote: 189
States carried: 16
Popular Vote: 21,991,292
Percentage: 45.1%

Opponent: Strom Thurmond
Home state: South Carolina
Party: Dixiecrat
Running Mate: Fielding L. Wright
Electoral Vote: 39
States carried: 4
Popular Vote: 1,175,930
Percentage: 2.

The Election of 1948

Nominee: Dwight David Eisenhower
Home State: Kansas
Party: Republican
Running Mate: Richard Nixon
Electoral Vote: 442
States Carried: 39
Popular Vote: 34,075,529
Percentage: 55.2%

Opponent: Adlai Stevenson
Home state: Illinois
Party: Democratic
Running Mate: John Sparkman
Electoral Vote: 89
States carried: 9
Popular Vote: 27,375,090
Percentage: 44.3%

Nominee: Dwight David Eisenhower
Home State: Kansas
Party: Republican
Running Mate: Richard Nixon
Electoral Vote: 457
States Carried: 41
Popular Vote: 35,579,180
Percentage: 57.4%

Opponent: Adlai Stevenson
Home state: Illinois
Party: Democratic
Running Mate: Estes Kefauver
Electoral Vote: 73
States carried: 7
Popular Vote: 26,028,028
Percentage: 42.0%

Nominee: John Fitzgerald Kennedy
Home State: Massachusetts
Party: Democratic
Running Mate: Lyndon Baines Johnson
Electoral Vote: 303
States Carried: 22
Popular Vote: 34,220,984
Percentage: 49.7%

Opponent: Richard Milhous Nixon
Home state: California
Party: Republican
Running Mate: Henry Cabot Lodge
Electoral Vote: 219
States carried: 26
Popular Vote: 34,108,157
Percentage: 49.6%

The Election of 1964
Nominee: Lyndon Baines Johnson
Home State: Texas
Party: Democratic
Running Mate: Hubert Humphrey
Electoral Vote: 486
States Carried: 44 + Washington D.C.
Popular Vote: 43,127,041
Percentage: 61.1%

Opponent: Barry Goldwater
Home state: Arizona
Party: Republican
Running Mate: William E. Miller
Electoral Vote: 52
States carried: 6
Popular Vote: 27,175,754
Percentage: 38.5%

Nominee: Richard Nixon
Home State: California
Party: Republican
Running Mate: Spiro Agnew
Electoral Vote: 301
States Carried: 32
Popular Vote: 31,783,783
Percentage: 43.4%

Opponent: Hubert Humphrey
Home state: Minnesota
Party: Democratic
Running Mate: Edmund Muskie
Electoral Vote: 191
States carried: 13
+Washington, D.C.
Popular Vote: 31,271,839
Percentage: 42.7%

Opponent: George Wallace
Home state: Alabama
Party: American Independent
Running Mate: Curtis LeMay
Electoral Vote: 46
States carried: 5
Popular Vote: 9,901,118
Percentage: 13.5%

The Election of 1972
Nominee: Richard Nixon
Home State: California
Party: Republican
Running Mate: Spiro Agnew
Electoral Vote: 520
States Carried: 49
Popular Vote: 47,168,710
Percentage: 60.7%

Opponent: George McGovern
Home state: South Dakota
Party: Democratic
Running Mate: Sargent Shriver
Electoral Vote: 17
States carried: 1
+Washington, D.C.
Popular Vote: 29,173,222
Percentage: 37.5%

Nominee: Jimmy Carter
Home State: Georgia
Party: Democratic
Running Mate: Walter Mondale
Electoral Vote: 297
States Carried: 23
+Washington, D.C.
Popular Vote: 40,831,881
Percentage: 50.1%

Opponent: Gerald Ford
Home state: Michigan
Party: Republican
Running Mate: Bob Dole
Electoral Vote: 240
States carried: 27
Popular Vote: 39,831,881
Percentage: 48.0%

The Election of 1980

Nominee: Ronal Reagan
Home State: California
Party: Republican
Running Mate: George H. W. Bush
Electoral Vote: 489
States Carried: 44
Popular Vote: 43,903,230
Percentage: 50.7%

Opponent: Jimmy Carter
Home state: Georgia
Party: Democratic
Running Mate: Walter Mondale
Electoral Vote: 49
States carried: 6
+Washington, D.C.
Popular Vote: 35,480,115
Percentage: 41.0%

The Election of 1984

Nominee: Ronald Wilson Reagan
Home State: California
Party: Democratic
Running Mate: George H. W. Bush
Electoral Vote: 525
States Carried: 49
Popular Vote: 54,455,472
Percentage: 58.8%

Opponent: Walter Mondale
Home state: Minnesota
Running Mate: Geraldine Ferraro
Electoral Vote: 13
States carried: 1
+Washington, D.C.
Popular Vote: 37,577,352
Percentage: 40.6%

The Election of 1988

Nominee: George H. W. Bush
Home State: Texas
Party: Republican
Running Mate: Dan Quayle
Electoral Vote: 426
States Carried: 40
Popular Vote: 48,886,597
Percentage: 53.4%

Opponent: Michael Dukakis
Home state: Massachusetts
Party: Democratic
Running Mate: Lloyd Bentsen
Electoral Vote: 111
States carried: 10
+Washington, D.C.
Popular Vote: 41,809,476
Percentage: 45.4%

The Election of 1992

Nominee: Bill Clinton
Home State: Arkansas
Party: Democratic
Running Mate: Al Gore
Electoral Vote: 370
States Carried: 32
+Washington, D.C.
Popular Vote: 44,909,806
Percentage: 43.0%

Opponent: George H. W. Bush
Home state: Texas
Party: Republican

Running Mate: Dan Quayle
Electoral Vote: 168
States carried: 18
Popular Vote: 39,104,500
Percentage: 37.7%

Opponent: Ross Perot
Home state: Texas
Party: Independent
Running Mate: James Stockdale
Electoral Vote: 0
States carried: 0
Popular Vote: 19,743,821
Percentage: 18.9%

The Election of 1996

Nominee: Bill Clinton
Home State: Arkansas
Party: Democratic
Running Mate: Al Gore
Electoral Vote: 379
States Carried: 31
+Washington, D.C.
Popular Vote: 47,402,357
Percentage: 49.24%

Opponent: Bob Dole
Home state: Kansas
Party: Republican
Running Mate: Jack Kemp
Electoral Vote: 159
States carried: 19
Popular Vote: 39,198,755
Percentage: 40.71%

The Election of 2000

Nominee: George W. Bush
Home State: Texas
Party: Republican
Running Mate: Dick Cheney
Electoral Vote: 271
States Carried: 30
Popular Vote: 50,456,002
Percentage: 47.9%

Opponent: Al Gore
Home state: Tennessee
Party: Democratic
Running Mate: Joe
Lieberman
Electoral Vote: 266
States carried: 20
+Washington, D.C.
Popular Vote: 50,999,897
Percentage: 48.4%

The Election of 2004

Nominee: George W. Bush
Home State: Texas
Party: Republican
Running Mate: Dick Cheney
Electoral Vote: 286
States Carried: 31
Popular Vote: 62,040,610
Percentage: 50.7%

Opponent: John Kerry
Home state: Massachusetts
Party: Democratic
Running Mate: John Edwards
Electoral Vote: 252
States carried: 19
+Washington, D.C.
Popular Vote: 59,028,444
Percentage: 48.3%

The Election of 2008

Nominee: Barack Obama
Home State: Illinois
Party: Democratic
Running Mate: Joe Biden
Electoral Vote: 365
States Carried: 28
+Washington, D.C. and
Nebraska's 2nd District
Popular Vote: 69,498,516
Percentage: 52.9%

Opponent: John McCain
Home state: Arizona
Party: Republican
Running Mate: Sarah Palin
Electoral Vote: 173
States carried: 22
Popular Vote: 59,948,323
Percentage: 45.7%

The Election of 2012

Nominee: Barack Obama
Home State: Illinois
Party: Democratic
Running Mate: Joe Biden
Electoral Vote: 332
States Carried: 26
+Washington, D.C.
Popular Vote: 65,915,796
Percentage: 51.1%

Opponent: Willard Mitt
Romney
Home state: Massachusetts
Party: Republican
Running Mate: Paul Ryan
Electoral Vote: 206
States carried: 24
Popular Vote: 60,933,500
Percentage: 47.2%

Introduction to Presidential Elections

Words to look for

Natural-born citizen   Eligible

Every four years there is a race to the White House—that is candidates vying to see who will win the presidency. But not everyone is qualified to be President of the United States. The qualifications, however, are simple and laid out in the United States Constitution in Article II, Section 1; it says:

No person except a natural born citizen, or a citizen of the United States, at the time of the adoption of this Constitution, shall be eligible to the office of President; neither shall any person be eligible to that office who shall not have attained to the age of thirty-five years, and been fourteen years a resident within the United States.

Every four years in the BIG race political parties and smaller and run to hold the highest elected Political parties are groups of because they have the same goal in mind—to elect a party to the presidency.

candidates from both of the major lesser known political parties position in our government. people who are bound together beliefs and have the same person from their political

Election Day takes place on first Monday in November every starts well before the general election.

the first Tuesday after the four years. But, the running

Candidates from many political parties for office. Then they go about trying to their political party so they can run in the

announce their candidacies win the nomination of general election.

The youngest person to take the office of president who was the sitting Vice President of the United William McKinley was assassinated. According to the succession laws, the Vice President then became president. Teddy Roosevelt was 42 years and 322 days old. The youngest person to be elected president was John Fitzgerald Kennedy at age 43 years and 236 days old.

was Theodore Roosevelt, States when President

The first campaigns did not resemble what we have now. In the first place it was considered to be beneath the candidates to go out and campaign for oneself. So, rival newspapers and advocates or surrogates did the campaigning on behalf of the candidates. That began to change in the mid-1800s when campaigns when political parties became more aggressive about trying to get their candidates elected.

The Presidents

George Washington

Born: February 22, 1732, Westmoreland County, Virginia
Died: December 14, 1799 (67 years old) Mount Vernon, Virginia
Married: Martha Dandridge Custis
Education: Tutored
Occupation: Farmer, Surveyor, Soldier
Religion: Anglican/Episcopalian
Party: None
Term: April 30, 1789, to March 3, 1797

John Adams

Born: October 30, 1735, Quincy Massachusetts
Died: July 4, 1826, (age 90) Quincy, Massachusetts
Married: Abigail Smith
Education: Harvard College
Occupation: Lawyer
Religion: Unitarian
Party: Federalist
Term: March 4, 1797 to March 4, 1801

Thomas Jefferson

Born: April 13, 1743, Shadwell, Virginia
Died: July 4, 1826, (83 years old) Monticello, Charlottesville, Virginia
Married: Martha Wayles Skelton
Education: The College of William and Mary
Occupation: Lawyer and farmer
Religion: Deist
Party: Democratic-Republican
Term: March 4, 1801, to March 4, 1809

James Madison

Born: March 16, 1751, Port Conway, Virginia
Died: June 28, 1836 (85 years old) Montpelier, Virginia
Married: Dolley Todd
Education: Princeton University
Occupation: Lawyer
Religion: Episcopalian
Party: Democratic-Republican
Term: March 4, 1809, to March 4, 1817

James Monroe

Born: April 28, 1758, Westmoreland County, Virginia
Died: July 4, 1831 (73 years old), New York, New York
Married: Elizabeth Kortright
Education: The College of William and Mary
Occupation: Farmer
Religion: Episcopalian
Party: Democratic-Republican
Term: March 4, 1817, to March 4, 1825

John Quincy Adams

Born: July 11, 1767, Braintree, Massachusetts
Died: February 23, 1848, (80 years old), Washington, D.C.
Married: Louisa Catherine Johnson
Education: Harvard College
Occupation: Lawyer
Religion: Unitarian
Party: Federalist
Term: March 4, 1825, to March 4, 1829

Andrew Jackson

Born: March 15, 1829, Lancaster County, South Carolina
Died: June 8, 1845 (78 years old), Nashville, Tennessee
Married: Rachel Donelson Robards
Education:
Occupation: Judge, farmer, soldier
Religion: Presbyterian
Party: Democratic-Republican, Democratic
Term: March 4, 1829, to march 4, 1837

Martin Van Buren

Born: December 5, 1782, Kinderhook, New York
Died: July 24, 1862 (79 years old) Kinderhook, New York
Married: Hannah Hoes
Education: Kinderhook Academy, studied for the New York Bar
Occupation: Lawyer
Religion: Dutch Reformed
Party: Democratic
Term: March4, 1837, to March 44, 1841

William Henry Harrison

Born: February 9, 1773, Charles City County, Virginia
Died: April 4, 1841 (68 years old), Washington, D.C.
Married: Anna Symmes
Education: University of Pennsylvania
Occupation: Soldier
Religion: Episcopalian
Party: Whig
Term: March 4, 1841, to April 4, 1841

John Tyler

Born: March 29, 1790, Charles City County, Virginia
Died: January 18, 1862 (71 years old), Richmond, Virginia
Married:
Letitia Christian (1st wife); Julia Gardiner (2nd wife)
Education: The College of William and Mary
Occupation: Lawyer
Religion: Episcopalian
Party: Whig
Term: April 4, 1841, to March 4, 1845

James Knox Polk

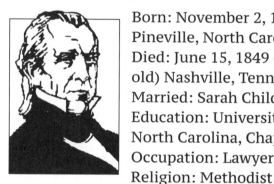

Born: November 2, 1795, Pineville, North Carolina
Died: June 15, 1849 (53 years old) Nashville, Tennessee
Married: Sarah Childress
Education: University of North Carolina, Chapel Hill
Occupation: Lawyer, farmer
Religion: Methodist
Party: Democratic
Term: March 4, 1845, to March 4, 1849

Zachary Taylor

Born: November 24, 1784, Barboursville, Virginia
Died: July 9, 1850 (65 years old) Washington, D.C.
Married: Margaret Smith
Education: privately tutored
Occupation: Soldier
Religion: Episcopalian
Party: Whig
Term: March 4, 1849, to July 9, 1850

Millard Fillmore

Born: January 7, 1800, Summerhill, New York
Died: March 8, 1874 (74 years old), Buffalo, New York
Married: Abigail Powers (1st wife); Caroline Carmichael (2nd wife)
Education: New Hope Academy
Occupation: Lawyer
Religion: Unitarian
Party: Whig
Term: July 9, 1850, to March 4, 1853

Franklin Pierce

Born: November 23, 1804, Hillsborough, New Hampshire
Died: October 8, 1869 (64 years old), Concord, New Hampshire
Married: Jane Appleton
Education: Bowdoin College
Occupation: Lawyer
Religion: Episcopalian
Party: Democratic
Term: March 4, 1853, to March 4, 1857

James Buchanan

Born: April 23, 1791, Mercersburg, Pennsylvania
Died: June 1, 1868 (71 years old) Lancaster, Pennsylvania
Married: Never
Education: Dickinson College
Occupation: Lawyer, diplomat
Religion: Presbyterian
Term: March 4, 1857, to March 4, 1861

Abraham Lincoln

Born: February 12, 1809, Hardin County, Kentucky
Died: April 15, 1865 (56 years old) Washington, D.C.
Married: Mary Todd
Education: Self taught
Occupation: Lawyer
Religion: No declared denomination.
Party: Republican
Term: March 4, 1861, to April 15, 1865

Andrew Johnson

Born: December 29, 1808, Raleigh, North Carolina
Died: July 31, 1875 (66 years old), Greenville, Tennessee
Married: Eliza McCardle
Education: Self taught and tutored
Occupation: Tailor
Religion: Christian (attended Methodist and Catholic services)
Party: Democratic
Term: April 15, 1865, to March 4, 1869

Ulysses S. Grant

Born: April 27, 1822, Point Pleasant, Ohio
Died: July 23, 1885, (63 years old) at Mount McGregor, New York
Married: Julia Dent
Education: U.S. Military Academy at West Point
Occupation: General, soldier
Religion: Methodist
Party: Republican
Term: March 4, 1869, to March 4, 1877

Rutherford Birchard Hayes

Born: October 4, 1822, Delaware, Ohio
Died: January 17, 1893, (70 years old), Fremont, Ohio
Married: Lucy Webb
Education: Harvard Law School
Occupation: Lawyer
Religion: Methodist
Party: Republican
Term: March 4, 1877, to March 4, 1881

James Abram Garfield

Born: November 19, 1831, Moreland Hills, Ohio
Died: September 19, 1881, (49 years old), Elberon (Long Branch), New Jersey
Married: Lucretia Rudolph
Education: Williams College
Occupation: Lawyer, teacher, minister
Religion: Republican
Party: Disciples of Christ
Term: March 4, 1881, to September 19, 1881

Chester A. Arthur

Born: October 5, 1829, Fairfield, Vermont
Died: November 18, 1886, (57 years old), New York, New York
Married: Ellen Lewis Herndon
Education: Union College, Schenectady, New York
Occupation: Lawyer, civil servant, teacher
Religion: Episcopalian
Party: Republican
Term: September 19, 1881, to March 4, 1885

Grover Cleveland

Born: March 18, 1837, Caldwell, New Jersey
Died: June 24, 1908, (71 years old), Princeton, New Jersey
Married: Francis Folsom
Education: self-taught for the New York Bar
Occupation: Lawyer, Governor
Religion: Presbyterian
Party: Democratic
Term: March 4, 1893, to March 4, 1897

Benjamin Harrison

Born: August 20, 1833, North Bend, Ohio
Died: March 13, 1901, (67 years old), Indianapolis, Indiana
Married: Caroline Scott (1st wife); Mary Scott Lord Dimmick (2nd wife)
Education: Miami University, Oxford, Ohio
Occupation: Lawyer
Religion: Presbyterian
Party: Republican
Term: March 4, 1889, to March 4, 1893

William McKinley

Born: January 29, 1843, Niles, Ohio
Died: September 14, 1901, (58 years old), Buffalo, New York
Married: Ida Sexton
Education: Albany Law School
Occupation: Lawyer
Religion: Methodist
Party: Republican
Term: March 4, 1897, to September 14, 1901

Theodore Roosevelt

Born: October 27, 1858, New York, New York
Died: January 6, 1919, (60 Years old), Oyster Bay, New York
Married: Alice Hathaway Lee (1st wife); Edith Kermit Carow (2nd wife)
Education: Columbia Law School, Harvard College
Occupation: Historian, civil servant
Religion: Dutch Reformed
Party: Republican
Term: September 14, 1901, to March 4, 1909

William Howard Taft

Born: September 15, 1857, Cincinnati, Ohio
Died: March 8, 1930, (72 years old), Washington, D.C.
Married: Helen Herron
Education: Yale University, University of Cincinnati
Occupation: Lawyer, Judge, Territorial Governor
Religion: Unitarian
Party: Republican
Term: March 4, 1909, to March 4, 1913

Woodrow Wilson

Born: December 28, 1856, Staunton, Virginia
Died: February 3, 1924, (67 years old), Washington, D.C.
Married: Ellen Axson (1st wife); Edith Galt (2nd wife)
Education: Princeton, University of Virginia
Occupation: Lawyer, College President
Religion: Presbyterian
Party: Democrat
Term: March 4, 1913, to March 4, 1921

Warren Gamaliel Harding

Born: November 2, 1865, near Blooming Grove, Ohio
Died: August 2, 1923 (53 years old), at San Francisco, California
Married: Florence King
Education: Ohio Central College
Occupation: Newspaperman
Religion: Baptist
Party: Republican
Term: March 4, 1921 to August 2, 1923

Calvin Coolidge

Born: July 4, 1872, Plymouth, Vermont
Died: January 5, 1933, (60 years old), Northampton, Massachusetts
Married: Grace Goodhue
Education: Amherst College
Occupation: Lawyer
Religion: Congregationalist
Party: Republican
Term: August 2, 1923 to March 4, 1929

Herbert Clark Hoover

Born: August 10, 1874, West Branch, Iowa
Died: October 20, 1964 (90 years old), New York, New York
Married: Lou Henry
Education: Stanford University
Occupation: Mining Engineer
Religion: Quaker
Party: Republican
Term: March 4, 1929 to March 4, 1933

Franklin Delano Roosevelt

Born: January 30, 1882 at Hyde Park, New York
Died: April 12, 1945 (63 years old) at Warm Spring, Georgia
Married: Eleanor Roosevelt
Education: Harvard University
Occupation: Lawyer
Religion: Episcopalian
Party: Democratic
Term: March 4, 1933 to April 12, 1945

Harry S Truman

Born: May 8, 1884, at Lamar, Missouri
Died: December 26, 1972 (88 years old), at Kansas City, Missouri
Married: Bess Wallace
Education: Kansas City Law School (didn't complete)
Occupation: Haberdasher, farmer
Religion: Baptist
Party: Democratic
Term: April 12, 1945 to January 20, 1953

Dwight David Eisenhower

Born: October 14, 1890 at Denison, Texas
Died: March 28, 1969 (78 years old), at Washington, D.C.
Married: Mamie Doud
Education: U.S. Military Academy at West Point
Occupation: Soldier
Religion: Presbyterian
Party: Republican
Term: January 20, 1953 to January 20, 1961

John Fitzgerald Kennedy

Born: May 29, 1917 at Brookline, Massachusetts
Died: November 22, 1963 (46 years old), at Dallas, Texas
Married: Jacqueline Lee Bouvier
Education: Harvard College
Occupation: Senator
Religion: Catholic
Party: Democratic
Term: January 20, 1961 to November 22, 1963

Lyndon Baines Johnson

Born: August 27, 1908 at Stonewall, Texas
Died: January 22, 1973 (64 years old) at Stonewall, Texas
Married: Claudia Taylor (Lady Bird)
Education: Southwest Texas State Teachers College
Occupation: Teacher, politician
Religion: Disciples of Christ
Party: Democratic
Term: November 22, 1963 to January 20, 1969

Richard Milhous Nixon

Born: January 9, 1969 at Yorba Linda, California
Died: April 22, 1994 (81 years old), at New York, New York
Married: Thelma Catherine "Pat" Ryan
Education: Whittier College, Duke University School of Law
Occupation: Lawyer, politician
Religion: Quaker
Party: Republican
Term: January 20, 1969 to August 9, 1974

Gerald Rudolf Ford

Born: July 14, 1913 at Omaha, Nebraska
Died: December 26, 2006 (93 years old), at Rancho Mirage, California
Married: Elizabeth "Betty" Bloomer Warren
Education: University of Michigan
Occupation: Lawyer
Religion: Episcopalian
Party: Republican
Term: August 9, 1974 to January 20, 1977

James "Jimmy" Earl Carter

Born: October 1, 1924 at Plains, Georgia
Died:
Married: Rosalynn Smith
Education: U.S. Naval Academy
Occupation: Peanut farmer, politician
Religion: Baptist
Party: Democrat
Term: January 20, 1977 to January 20, 1981

Ronald Wilson Reagan

Born: February 6, 1911 at Tampico, Illinois
Died: June 5, 2005 (93 years old) at Bel Air, Los Angeles, California
Married: Jane Wyman (1st wife), Nancy Davis (2nd wife)
Education: Eureka College
Occupation: Actor, politician
Religion: Presbyterian
Party: Republican
Term: January 20, 1981 to January 20, 1989

George Herbert Walker Bush

Born: June 12, 1924 at Milton, Massachusetts
Died:
Married: Barbara Pierce
Education: Yale University
Occupation: Oil businessman
Religion: Episcopalian
Party: Republican
Term: January 20, 1989 to January 20, 1993

William "Bill" Jefferson Clinton

Born: August 19, 1946 at Hope, Arkansas
Died:
Married: Hillary Rodham
Education: Georgetown University; University College at Oxford; Yale Law School
Occupation: Lawyer, politician
Religion: Baptist
Party: Democratic
Term: January 20, 1993 to January 20, 2001

George Walker Bush

Born: July 6, 1946 at New Haven, Connecticut
Died:
Married: Laura Welch
Education: Yale University; Harvard Business School
Occupation: Oil and Baseball Businessman
Religion: United Methodist
Party: Republican
Term: January 20, 2001 to January 20, 2009

Barrack Hussein Obama

Born: August 4, 1961 at Honolulu,
Hawaii
Died:
Married: Michelle Robinson
Education: Columbia University;
Harvard Law School
Occupation: Law professor,
community organizer
Religion: Christian
Party: Democratic
Term: January 20, 2001 to

Project: The Budget

Build your own Presidential Campaign as a group project. First, allow students to chose their Campaign Manager. Explain that whenever there is something as important and as big as a Presidential campaign, there is always a budget. The budget organizes how much money will be spent on the campaign in all facets. Have students review chapter On The Campaign Trail (page 26). Copy the real budget and sample pages. Guided by each Campaign Manager, have each group develop their own.

The Look and Message of the Campaign

Explain that the look and message of the campaign must be consistent. Look at the back cover of this book to give you ideas of campaign buttons, slogans and designs.

Opinion Polls Chapter on page 56.

Each group's campaign manager will designate members to design the ads, billboards, magazine ads, postcards, .30 second tv ad, and so on. Others will be responsible for writing copy including a radio ad. Use the templates enclosed as a media guides.

The campaign manager will oversee all production of the campaign. And, most important, they will make sure that the look, message and platform remain consistent.

All campaign managers will present their group's campaign to the class.

Each group will recreate an opinion poll related to their candidate. Pollsters will query students who reviewed another group's campaign. (see Chapter 12 for direction.)

Optional

* Think about designating a student from each group to act as political candidates and put on a debate based on the campaign platform.

*Students could vote for their favorite candidates by making voting cards and voting booths.

Postcard

Postcards are very much like billboards in that there is not as much that you are able to write. Keep your message short and succinct. Perhaps highlight one idea. Always use the same design in your advertising campaign to keep your candidate's brand recognizable. Postcards (8.5 x 5.5) vertical or horizontal.

Billboard

Billboards are huge advertising spaces. The art and message on these billboards should be very simple and short. Theoretically, it takes 3 or 4 seconds to read the messages on the billboards. Any more than that is not only poor advertising but dangerous for a driver on the road. (Reduced size to 12" x 6" vertical, or proportionatly smaller as below)

Direct Mail

Always use the candidates slogans, picture and logo design in a direct mail campaign. In addition to information on the candidate, incorporate the candidates platform and vision of how he or she will change things. Think about what the message that you want your candidate to get across or target to special interest groups. Brochure — 8.5" x 11"- 2 folds

Storyboard for TV spot

Creating a TV ad always begins with a storyboard. Director's use storyboards to plot out the angles of the camera and what the actor, in this case, candidate will say within the 30 seconds they have to give their message.

Draw a scene in each panel of how you envision your commercial to look and what your candidate will say. Study other commercials to see how they work. Write copy that includes the narrator, your candidate and the slogan. Read the script aloud and time it to be 30 seconds.

Slogan_____

Key: Understanding the storyboard language.
Duration: The length of the camera filming on the subject.
Shot: Various camera angles-Wide shot, Close up, Long Shot, Medium shot, Extreme Close Up.
Audio1: Music, sound effects. **Audio 2:** Voice over (narrator) and/or dialog (Candidate)
Transition: (Changing from one scene to the next) Dissolve, cut, quick cuts)

Radio Script

Type out what you want your candidate to say. Perhaps you will have another person give a testimonial about your candidate. Or, have the candidate try to influence the audience to vote. Either way, you only have 30 seconds to give a strong message.

Write a commercial statement on each line.

30 second spot for candidate (name) _____

MUSIC: 03 seconds (music choice) _____

Announcer: (Time) _____

_____

_____

Candidate (Time) _____

_____

_____

_____

Announcer: (Time) _____

_____

_____

Candidate (Time) _____

_____

_____

_____

Announcer: (Time) _____

_____

_____

MUSIC: 03 seconds (music choice) _____

Building a Platform with Planks

Objective: Students will learn how to make platforms or declarations that are the foundation of each party. By generating questions in small groups, students will recall information, ask questions, and explore topics in depth. See Chapter 15 for a comparison of platforms and planks on project page 102 &103.

1. Access student's prior knowledge by asking them to share what they know about each political party.

Explain that the platforms are the political party's principles; and, the public policy or goals that are established by the party are known as "planks" that speak to a variety of issues.

Some planks appeal to special interest groups.

2. Ask: Which special interest groups inform the planks for both parties?

3. Designate teams and have students research the current platforms and planks of each party.

Pick just a few favorites and write them down.

Democratic platform and planks

_____

_____

_____

Republican platform and planks

_____

_____

_____

_____

_____

4. Copy as many "plank" designs you need for each party. Color light brown or yellow.

5. Copy one Democratic platform design and one Republican platform. Color light brown or yellow

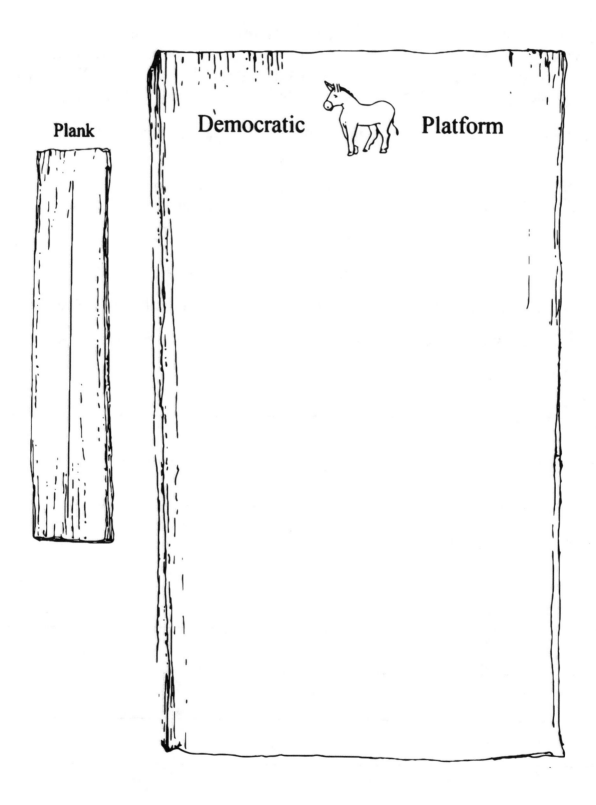

Plank

Democratic Platform

Race to the White House: **ELECTING THE PRESIDENT**

6. Write in each plank for each party. Glue onto the specific party platform design.

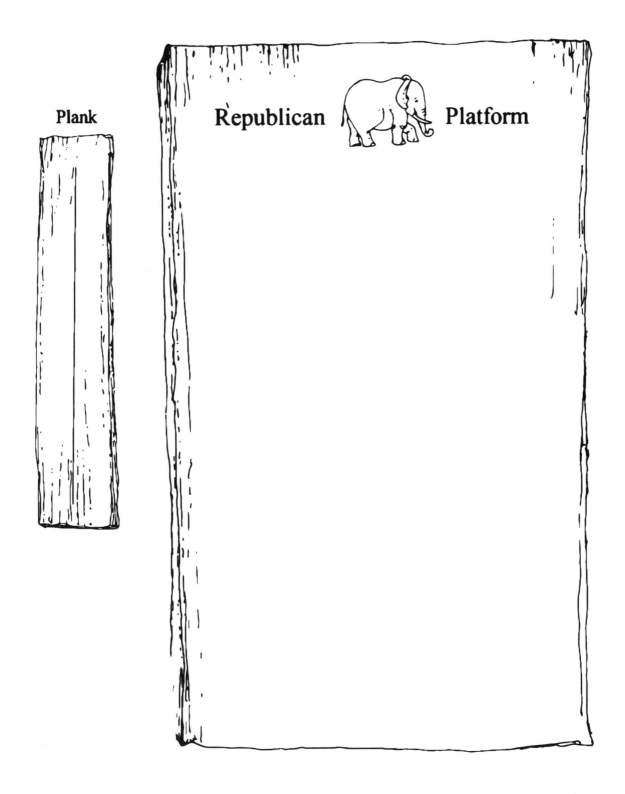

Plank

Republican Platform

Project 2
The Campaign Game

You can play with 2 to 4 players. The first person that follows the Campaign Trail board around to the White House wins the presidency. Students should have studied the Glossary terms in the back of the book.

You need a pair of die and up to 4 players

1. Markers: Copy the Candidate form (right) on index or heavy paper. Cut out and fold on bottom line.

Then cut out current presidential candidates images from magazines or copy past president's images in this book (pages 88-95). Copy one candidate form onto index paper and paste your presidential candidate onto the form.

Cut out the form

2. Campaign Trail Board: Enlarge and copy the Campaign Trail Board to ledger size. Color and decorate (following page).

3. Copy the Glossary words and their definitions on pages 109-110. Cut out the words and terms and fold the strips. Place all folded strips in a bowl.

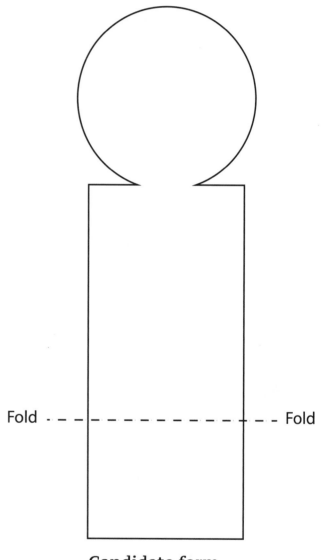

Fold - - - - - - - - - - - - - - Fold

Candidate form

How to play

1. Roll the die to see who goes first. Place their candidate form markers on "The Soap Box" to start.

2. Students play the game by counting the spaces with each roll of the dice. Go around the board and follow the instructions in each space.

Rules

Every player is a candidate and must follow the path to the presidency. The first candidate to reach the Whitehouse wins.

Follow the steps in each space. They will determine what to do for each turn.

Extra points

Glossary words and their definitions: Landing on a Glossary word space means the possibility of advancing forward on the board by 5 extra spaces if answered correctly!

When a player lands on a Glossary Word space, they pull one folded glossary/definition slip from pile then hands it to player on left. The player to the left reads the glossary definition while the player must answer with the correct word. If answered correctly, the player moves 5 spaces.

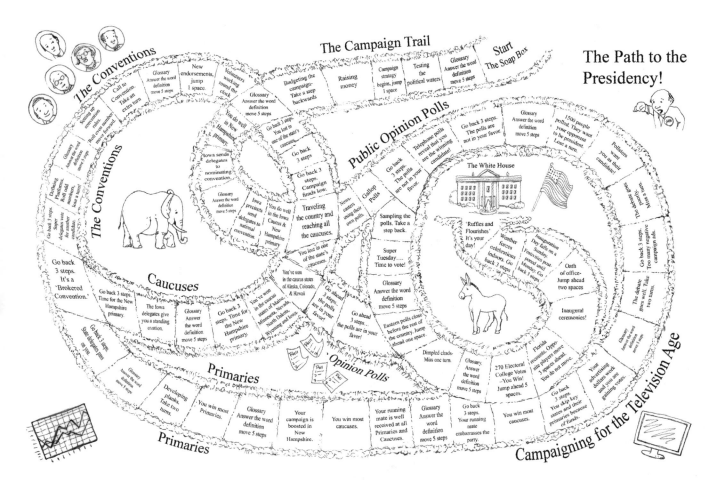

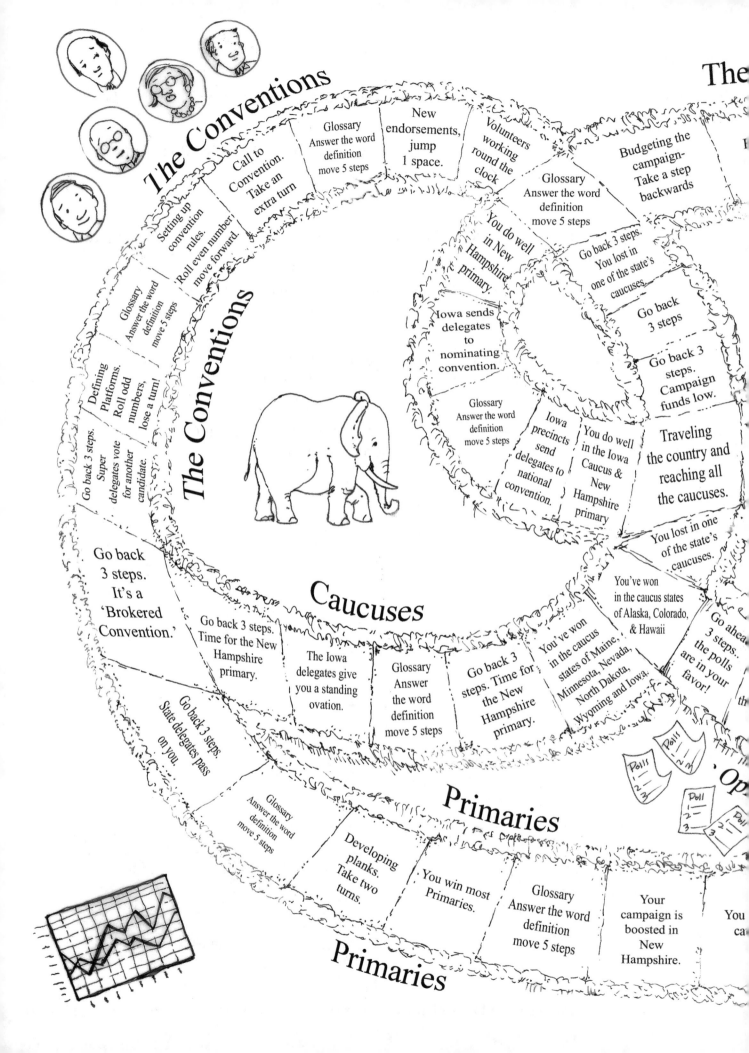

The Conventions

The Conventions

The Conventions

Caucuses

Primaries

Primaries

The

Op

Outer ring (The Conventions):

Call to Convention. Take an extra turn

Glossary Answer the word definition move 5 steps

New endorsements, jump 1 space.

Volunteers working round the clock

Glossary Answer the word definition move 5 steps

Budgeting the campaign- Take a step backwards

Setting up convention rules. Roll even number, move forward.

Glossary Answer the word definition move 5 steps

Defining Platforms. Roll odd numbers, lose a turn!

Go back 3 steps. Super delegates vote for another candidate.

Go back 3 steps. It's a 'Brokered Convention.'

Go back 3 steps. Time for the New Hampshire primary.

The Iowa delegates give you a standing ovation.

Glossary Answer the word definition move 5 steps

Go back 3 steps. Time for the New Hampshire primary.

You've won in the caucus states of Maine, Nevada, Minnesota, North Dakota, Wyoming and Iowa.

Go ahead 3 steps. the polls are in your favor!

Go back 3 steps. State delegates pass on you.

Glossary Answer the word definition move 5 steps

Developing planks. Take two turns.

You win most Primaries.

Glossary Answer the word definition move 5 steps

Your campaign is boosted in New Hampshire.

You ca

Inner ring (Caucuses):

You do well in New Hampshire primary.

Glossary Answer the word definition move 5 steps

Go back 3 steps. You lost in one of the state's caucuses.

Go back 3 steps

Go back 3 steps. Campaign funds low.

Iowa sends delegates to nominating convention.

Iowa precincts send delegates to national convention.

You do well in the Iowa Caucus & New Hampshire primary

Traveling the country and reaching all the caucuses.

You lost in one of the state's caucuses.

You've won in the caucus states of Alaska, Colorado, & Hawaii

The Path to the Presidency!

aign Trail

Campaign strategy egins, jump 1 space

Testing the political waters

Glossary Answer the word definition move 5 steps

Start
The Soap Box

Opinion Polls

Go back 3 steps. The polls are not in your favor.

Glossary Answer the word definition move 5 steps

1500 people polled. They want your opponent to be president. Lose a turn.

Telephone polls reveal that you are the winning candidate!

Pollsters want you as their candidate!

Go back 3 steps. The polls are not in your favor.

The debate goes poorly. Miss a turn.

Go back 3 steps. Too many negative campaign ads.

The White House

Sampling the polls. Take a step back.

'Ruffles and Flourishes' It's your day!

Weather forces celebrations indoors. Go back 3 steps

Inauguration Day falls on a Sunday. Festivities post-poned until Monday. Go back 3 steps.

Oath of office-Jump ahead two spaces

The debate goes well. Take two turns.

Super Tuesday.... me to vote!

Glossary swer the word definition move 5 steps

Inaugural ceremonies!

Glossary Answer the word definition move 5 steps

Eastern polls close before the rest of the country. Jump ahead one space.

Florida recounts. Oppo-site players move 3 spaces ahead. You do not move.

Dimpled chads- Miss one turn.

Glossary. Answer the word definition move 5 steps

270 Electoral College Votes –You Win! Jump ahead 5 spaces.

Your advertising dollars work and you are gaining votes.

Go back 3 steps. You skip key states and their primaries because of funds.

lls

our running ate is well ceived at all rimaries and Caucuses.

Glossary Answer the word definition move 5 steps

Go back 3 steps. Your running mate embarrasses the party.

You win most caucuses.

Campaigning for the Television Age

Glossary

Balance: When a presidential candidate and party look for a vice-presidential candidate who is able to bring additional voters that the presidential candidate could not.

Cabinet- A group of individuals who advise the president.

Canvas: When individuals from a campaign team knock on doors or phone in order to persuade voters to cast their ballots for their candidates on Election Day.

Catch phrases: Short expressions or phrases that are used often because of its importance.

Chads: A small piece of paper that should be removed when punched through a ballot with a machine during the voting process.

Certified: An official confirmation of a person, object or organization that is given some sort of review or assessment.

Concession statement: In politics it is the statement when the losing candidate publicly yields or quits to the winning candidate.

Congressional Representatives: A person who represents the people in the various districts of each state.

Convention: A huge political meeting where platforms are developed and candidates are chosen for upcoming elections

Delegate: Someone who speaks on behalf of a political party during a national convention.

Demeanor: The way a person appears to behave from someone else's point of view.

Elect: The process of selecting a person for public office by voting.

Electoral college: The institution that officially elects the president by votes from delegates and not by the popular vote.

Emancipated: Freed from the control of another person or system such as slavery.

Fanfair: A short or elaborate display of pomp during Election Day.

Front-porch: A low-key presidential campaign in which the candidate remains at home or closeto home during the campaign.

Frontrunner: A term that describes the leader in a race

Graft: A form of political corruption.

Horse-trading: Bargaining or making excellent political deals.

Inauguration: A formal ceremony and 'swearing in' that marks the beginning of a President and Vice President's four-year term in office.

Incumbent: An elected official who holds a political office

Jim Crow Laws: Segregation laws that were enacted after the Civil War and into the Reconstruction period of the Southern states.

Junkets: Trips taken by politicians for official reasons.

Lame Duck: A President who is approaching the end of the term and has less influence over politicians because there is little time left in office.

Mandate: A command or authorization given by an elected official.

Media: Usually referring to radio, television, newspapers, magazines and so on.

Mudslinging: Insulting someone or trying to ruin a reputation.

Muster-up: To gather up with some difficulty.

Planks: A term that represents the list of actions, goals and proposals of a platform that is supported by political parties and Presidential candidates.

Platform: During a political convention, delegates develop a series of statements and principles. Each platform is made up of goals or proposals known as "planks". Political parties and Presidential Candidates use these platforms as a part of their campaign.

Political analyst: A person who is involved in raising awareness of certain political issues.

Pollsters: Someone who asks questions and gathers answers in a poll.

President-elect: The term used for an incoming President who has not yet taken office.

Rallies: A gathering of people with similar beliefs who listen to political speakers. Political rallies are often events that are used to raise money and support while maintaining high energy and excitement.

Ratified: To officially agree to something by signing or voting.

Reconstruction: The reorganization of the Southern states after the Civil War.

Resignation: The formal act of quitting a position or important office.

Restore: To put back into an original state.

Running mate: A term that describes the Vice-Presidential candidate during a campaign.

Sampling: A select amount of people surveyed for a poll. The sampled group reflects the opinions of a larger group.

Statistical modeling: An idealized form of assumptions concerning data that is gathered from a large population. Often used in developing samples for polls.

Strategy or Strategic planning: Techniques or tactics that are used in nearly every political campaign for the purpose of getting a candidate elected.

Straw polls: Unofficial vote.

Super delegate: A delegate in a political party who is either a party leader or elected official.

Theory of Probability: The mathematical determination of random events and quantities.

Super Tuesday: The Tuesday that is designated in February and March in which the political parties hold their primary elections to select their presidential candidates.

Ticket: The listing of the residential and vice presidential candidates on the same ballot.

Town hall meetings: Informal public meetings political figures use to propose new ideas.

Unbiased: Free from any prejudice or favoritism.

Watergate: A hotel in Washington, D.C. where a major political scandal began in 1972.

Whistle-stop: A type of touring political campaign in which a candidate makes a series of brief appearances or speeches on the open platform of a railcar.

Answer Key

Introduction to Presidential elections

Page 8 – Review 1:

1. 35 years old, natural born citizen, has to have lived in the United States for the previous 14 years.

2. Candidates gave speeches, handed out posters, issued campaign buttons, and participated in torch-light parades.

3. Theodore Roosevelt.

4. John Fitzgerald Kennedy

5. Theodore Roosevelt became president upon the death of William McKinley. He was older than Kennedy when Kennedy was elected president.

Page 9 – Activity 2: Identify that Slogan

A. "Four more years of the full dinner pail" 1904 – William McKinley

B. "A Chicken in every pot and a car in every garage" 1928 _ Herbert Hoover

Activity 3: Match that Slogan to the Presidential Campaign

C. (Harry S Truman 2. D. Theodore Roosevelt 3. A. Franklin Delano Roosevelt 4. B. Alfred M. Landon

Page 12 – Who is Eligible to Be President?

Review: 1. (g) (A). John McCain was born on a military base considered a possession of the United States with a parent serving honorably in the United States Navy. 2. (a) a person born in the United States and subject to the jurisdiction thereof. Hawaii is part of the United States being one of the 50 states and therefore makes him a natural born citizen.

Page 15 – The Oath of Office and the responsibilities of the President

1. The Constitution does not define who should swear in the President. However, by tradition, the person is usually the Chief Justice of the United States Supreme Court

2. Answers will vary but might include: an oath is a pledge to do something. In this case, to defend and uphold the Constitution of the United States

3. Legislative, Judicial and Executive

4. Act as commander in Chief, sign or veto laws, negotiate treaties, and appoint judges and ambassadors.

5. Chief Executive manages the Executive Branch of the government.

Page 17 – Term Limits

1. Two terms

2. 22 Amendment

3. George Washington

4. Franklin Delano Rossevelt

5. According to Section 1 of the 22nd Amendment if a person has served more than two years can be elected to the presidency more than once. Therefore if a president died in office in less than one year in office, the successor would serve more than two years before the next election and would only be eligible to serve one elected term.

Page 21 – Voting Laws Then and Now

1. Answers will vary

2. Answers will vary

3. Answers will vary

4. Answers will vary

Page 24 – Political Parties Review

1. No, George Washington did not belong to a political party

2. Federalist, Democratic-Republican, Democrat, Republican and Whig

3. Democratic Party

4. William Henry Harrison, john Tyler, Zachary Taylor, Millard Fillmore

5. Republican

6. George Washington in his Farwell Address

7. John Adams

Page 27 – Political Parties: Thomas Nast Political Cartoon

1. Nast created the symbols for the Democratic and Republican Parties and they appear for the first time together in this political cartoon.

2. Delaware Senator Thomas Bayard is the Democrat—he is holding the tail of the donkey, the symbol of the Democratic Party.

Secretary Of The Treasury John Sherman is the Republican—he is standing next to the elephant, the symbol for the Republican Party

4. Nast depicts the Democratic position of returning to the gold standard as jumping into chaos.

5. Neither.

Page 35 – First in the Nation: The Iowa Caucus and the New Hampshire Primary Political Cartoon Handout

1. People gather in groups demonstrating their support.

2. The primary is a secret ballot, caucus are where voting is done by moving from one group to another as a show of support for a candidate.

3. Every four years in Iowa.

4. Every four years in New Hampshire.

Page 37

1. In a caucus voters gather in groups to publically declare their support for a candidate. In a primary, the balloting is done in secret.

2. Iowa

3. New Hampshire

4. Because the cartoonist is making the point that in the election of the president these two political contest are the most important and little else matters up to that point.

5. That the Iowa caucuses and the New Hampshire primary is blown out of portion compared to the other political contests in the United States. And during the early election season only two states matter and loom large in picking the candidate from each party to be the nominee.

Page 44 – The Conventions Review

1. Answers will vary

2. Answers will vary

3. Answers will vary

Page 47 – Project: Presidential Picks Crossword Puzzle

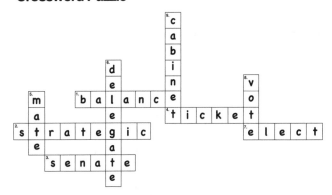

Page 51 – Project: Collect and Analyze Campaign Ephemera

A.

1. Answers will vary

2. Answers will vary

3. Answers will vary

4. Answers will vary

B.

1. Answers will vary

2. Answers will vary

3. Answers will vary

4. Answers will vary

5. Answers will vary

6. Answers will vary

7. Answers will vary

Page 70 – Project

1. Answers will vary

2. Answers will vary

3. Answers will vary

4. Answers will vary

5. Answers will vary

6. Answers will vary

Page 74

1. January 20th at 12 noon.

2. Drums and bugles

3. Presidents and Vice-Presidents are sworn into office in a private ceremony. The public ceremony is held the following day.

4. Chief Justice

5. "Hail to the Chief"

6. "Hail Columbia"

7. Mid term, if the past president has passed away, incapacitated or impeached.

8. 21-gun salutes

9. The swearing-in ceremony